DISTURBING THE PEACE

DISTURBING THE PEACE

Václav Havel was born in Czechoslovakia in 1936. Among his plays, those best known in the West are *The Garden Party*, *The Increased Difficulty of Concentration*, *The Memorandum*, *Largo Desolato*, *Temptation*, and three one-act plays: *Audience*, *Private View*, and *Protest*. He is a founding spokesman of Charter 77 and the author of many influential essays on the nature of totalitarianism and dissent, including 'An Open Letter to Dr Husák' and 'The Power of the Powerless'. In 1979 he was sentenced to four and a half years in prison for his involvement in the Czech human rights movement; out of this imprisonment came his book of letters to his wife, *Letters to Olga* (1988). In January 1983, for reasons of health, he was released from prison before his sentence was completed. In 1986 he was awarded the Erasmus Prize, the highest cultural award in the Netherlands. In November 1989 he helped to found the Civic Forum, the first legal opposition movement in Czechoslovakia in forty years; and in December 1989 he was elected President of Czechoslovakia.

Karel Hvížďala is a Czech journalist and playwright living in West Germany. *Disturbing the Peace* is one of a series of book-length interviews he has conducted with important figures from Czechoslovak political and cultural life.

Paul Wilson lived in Czechoslovakia for ten years, working as a translator and English teacher and playing with an underground rock band, the Plastic People of the Universe. He was expelled in 1977. He has translated several Czech writers, including Josef Škvorecký and Bohumil Hrabal. He is the co-author of a series of radio documentaries on Eastern Europe for the Canadian Broadcasting Corporation. He is an associate editor of the *Idler* magazine in Toronto, where he lives.

Disturbing the Peace

A Conversation with
Karel Hvížďala

VÁCLAV HAVEL

Translated from the Czech and with
an introduction by Paul Wilson

faber and faber
LONDON · BOSTON

First published in the USA in 1990
by Alfred A. Knopf, Inc.,
and simultaneously in Canada by Random House of Canada Limited, Toronto
This export paperback edition first published in Great Britain in 1990
by Faber and Faber Limited
3 Queen Square London WC1N 3AU

Published in Germany as *Fernverhör* by Rowohlt Verlag GmbH, Reinbek bei
Hamburg in 1987
Copyright © 1987 by Rowohlt Verlag GmbH, Reinbek bei Hamburg
Dálkový výslech © 1986 by Václav Havel
Published by arrangement with Rowohlt Verlag GmbH, Reinbek bei Hamburg
Published in Czech by Rozmluvy in 1986

Grateful acknowledgement is made to Unwin Hyman Ltd. for permission to reprint
an excerpt from *Charter 77 and Human Rights in Czechoslovakia* by H. Gordon Skilling.
Reprinted by kind permission of Unwin Hyman Ltd.

Portions of this work were originally published in the *New York Review of Books*

Printed in England by Clays Ltd, St Ives plc

Translation © Paul Wilson, 1990

A CIP record of this book is available
from the British Library
ISBN 0-571-14362-8

Contents

Preface

The history of this book has been marked by history itself.

When Karel Hvížďala first proposed the idea of a book-length interview to Václav Havel in 1985, Hvížďala was living in West Germany, Havel in Prague, and neither of them could visit the other. Havel liked the idea because it would give him a chance to reflect on his life as he approached fifty; he accepted. They worked on the book over the next year, communicating by underground mail. According to Hvížďala, the first approach, in which Havel sent written responses to the questions, did not satisfy either of them: the answers were too much like essays. So Hvížďala sent Havel a batch of about fifty questions, and between Christmas and the New Year, Havel shut himself in a borrowed flat and came out with eleven hours of recorded answers. Hvížďala transcribed and edited them, then sent the manuscript back to Havel with some supplementary questions ("for drama," Hvížďala says). Havel prepared a final version with some new material in it, completing it in early June, 1986.

The book was first published in Prague that same summer under Havel's own samizdat imprint, *Edice Expedice*. In autumn, a Czech emigré publishing venture in England, Rozmluvy, brought it out in the West. In December 1989— with Czechoslovakia's democratic revolution barely a few weeks old—the Melantrich Press in Prague had it published

in seven days. It was the first samizdat book to come out le-
gally in the new Czechoslovakia.

Translating this book was one of the most enjoyable tasks
I've ever undertaken. Havel had said it would be "recreation"
after the hard labor of *Letters to Olga,* and he was right. I
followed his method of composition, translating it first into
a tape recorder, and then editing the transcript. I'm not sure
it was any faster that way, but I hope the result has something
of the quality of Havel's conversation in it.

The Czech title of this book is *Dálkový výslech,* which means
Long-Distance Interrogation. For a long time, this title stood over
my translation too; it was awkward but accurate, and something of the irony of the original does seep through. Then
somewhere in the higher councils of publishing, doubts were
cast upon the title, and the search for a new one began.

My mind acknowledged the need for a different title, but
it refused to work on the problem. Then one day Bobbie
Bristol phoned from Knopf and said, "How do you feel about
disturbing the peace?" I thought she was suggesting another
late-night turn through the Lower East Side (such as we'd had
on my last New York trip) ending up in Dan Lynch's bar on
Second Avenue. No, she was suggesting a title. It was an in-
triguing idea: "disturbing the peace" was how I once translated the expression *výtržnictví,* a crime normally rendered as
"hooliganism," for which my friend Ivan Jirous (and many
others too) had been sent to prison. Jirous later wrote that he
liked my translation because it described exactly what he had
done: disturbed the artificial "peace" of the totalitarian system. Although Havel was once charged with *výtržnictví,* he was
never successfully prosecuted for it; nevertheless disturbing
the peace was, in a sense, what he had been doing all along:
disturbing the emperor's peace of mind. So the title—not
without some debate—was chosen and ultimately cleared with
Havel.

There may be purists who object to such negotiations, but
it doesn't hurt to remind ourselves that a book, and especially
a translation, is a collective creation. I would like to thank

everyone who, knowingly or unknowingly, helped in the completion of this work. I am grateful to Ivan and Dáša Havel, and Olga Havlová for many kindnesses; to Vladimír Hanzel for giving me time when there was none to give; and to the author himself for patiently dealing with my queries in the middle of a revolution. On this end, my thanks go especially to Marcy Laufer, for her prompt and reliable transcripts; to Bobbie Bristol, for far more than the title; to Edwin C. Cohen, for expressing his admiration of Václav Havel in the most direct way possible: by contributing to the translation fee; and to my wife Helena, for putting up with me while I finished the work under the pressure of history. As it turned out, it was a history which this book, in part, helped to unleash.

Paul Wilson

Introduction

In the spring of 1975, outside the Slavia Café, just across the street from the National Theatre in Prague, a friend handed me a well-thumbed sheaf of typewritten pages and told me to pass it on when I was through. In the real-life paranoia of Czechoslovakia in the 1970s, our encounter had a touch of conspiracy about it: reading or possessing samizdat—self-published works—was not illegal in itself, but circulating it was, and the two of us had just committed a crime. Our chances of being caught were slim, but still real enough to induce a sense of caution in us and add some salt and pepper to the moment. That evening, at home, I sat down to read in a state of excitement that only the knowledge of doing something illicit can bring.

It was an extraordinary essay, addressed to the Czechoslovak president, Gustav Husák, about the desolate state of the country seven years after the Warsaw Pact armies had crushed the Prague Spring. The author described a society governed by fear—not the cold, pit-of-the-stomach terror that Stalin had once spread throughout his empire, but a dull, existential fear that seeped into every crack and crevice of daily life and made one think twice about everything one said and did. This fear was maintained by the Secret Police, "that hideous spider whose invisible web runs right through society," and it reduced human action—and therefore history itself—to false pretense.

The letter was, in fact, a state of the union message, and it contained an unforgettable metaphor: the regime, the author said, was "entropic," a force that was gradually reducing the vital energy, diversity, and unpredictability of Czechoslovak society to a state of dull, inert uniformity. And the letter also contained a remarkable prediction: that sooner or later, this regime would become the victim of its own "lethal principle." "Life cannot be destroyed for good," the author wrote. "A secret streamlet trickles on beneath the heavy crust of inertia and pseudo-events, slowly and inconspicuously undermining it. It may be a long process, but one day it has to happen: the crust can no longer hold and starts to crack. This is the moment when something once more begins visibly to happen, something new and unique.... History again demands to be heard."

The letter, dated April 8, 1975, was signed "Václav Havel, Writer."

Havel finished this autobiographical interview with Karel Hvížďala in 1986. As I read it again, in the spring of 1990, I am struck by how the extraordinary events of the last few months—events that have toppled communist regimes from Berlin to Bucharest and that have borne the playwright Václav Havel from the ghetto of dissent to the world stage—have enriched it with new levels of meaning. Havel, for instance, describes in detail the struggle, in the mid-sixties, to keep a small literary magazine, *Tvář*, alive in the face of pressure from the Communist Party to close it down. In this struggle, Havel discovered what he called "a new model of behavior": when arguing with a center of power, don't get sidetracked into vague ideological debates about who is right or wrong; fight for specific, concrete things, and be prepared to stick to your guns to the end.

On Tuesday morning, November 28, 1989, Havel led a delegation of the Civic Forum to negotiate with the Communist-dominated government. The issue was not a magazine this time, it was the country. Ten days before that, the "velvet revolution" had been set in motion by a student demonstration in Prague; that was followed by a week of massive demonstrations culminating in a general strike on Monday, November 27. Early Tuesday afternoon, following the meeting, the government announced that it had agreed to write the leading role of the Communist Party out of the constitution. We do not know what was said at the meeting, but I don't think we would be far wrong to assume that the discussion stayed very close to the concrete issue of amending the constitution, and that the Civic Forum delegation stuck to their guns. A principle that Havel and his colleagues had learned decades before now stood them in good stead.

The parallels run deeper still. Havel's description of the birth of Charter 77 in 1977 is an almost uncanny prefiguration of the creation—in radically different circumstances—of the Civic Forum itself. Although for legal reasons it was described as an "initiative" and avoided making overt political proposals, Charter 77 was in fact a political movement in the deepest sense, a coalition of many groups of people from widely different backgrounds, ranging from former party members who still thought of themselves as Marxists to noncommunists who had never had anything to do with the party (except perhaps as its victims), but who all agreed on the fundamental importance of openness, tolerance, and respect for human rights. Havel describes the plurality of the Charter as something historically new for Czechoslovakia, something that would germinate a genuine social tolerance. Regardless of how it turned out, this achievement could not be wiped out of the national memory. "It was a stepping out toward life," he says, "toward a genuine state of thinking about common matters ... and the cost of doing so was saying goodbye forever to the principle of 'the leading role of the party.'"

In one sense, the Civic Forum, the creation of which Havel announced on November 19th in the Činoherní Klub in Prague, was Charter 77 writ large. Like the Charter, it was a coalition of all the forces in society (and by 1989 there were many) that had sought a nonviolent, nonpartisan solution to the crisis. The Civic Forum's program, called "What We Want" and issued only a week later, was drafted by, among others, Charter signatories; it strongly reflected the discussions that Charter 77 and other civic groups had been carrying on among themselves for the previous thirteen years. Moreover, the Forum's miraculous ability to act quickly, to make rapid decisions, to organize efficiently (despite appearing utterly chaotic), and to communicate effectively was possible largely thanks to the wide network built up over the years in difficult conditions among dissident and quasi-dissident groups. The atmosphere of those chaotic, exhilarating early days of revolution in November and December (so vividly described by Timothy Garton Ash in *The New York Review of Books*, and reprinted in his new book, *The Magic Lantern*) is anticipated in miniature by Havel's account of the early days of Charter 77, when his flat, as he said, "began to look suspiciously the way the New York Stock Exchange must have looked during the crash of '29, or like some center of revolution." There was a big difference, though: in 1977, the "hideous spider" was weaving its web tightly around the Chartists: in 1989, the spider had withdrawn, and the nation was beginning the enormous task of disentangling itself.

Disturbing the Peace, though, offers far more than insights into Havel the President, Havel the first among equals in a democracy struggling courageously to be reborn. It is a detailed and complex self-portrait of a man who sees himself both as an ordinary person, with down-to-earth needs and desires and aspirations and humors (he once said that the reason he was never tempted to emigrate was that he was just a Czech bumpkin at heart and he liked it there) and as someone whose destiny is interwoven with the destiny of his country. Havel, the writer by choice who became a politician *malgré lui,* has literally written himself into his country's history. His power as a writer and his power as a politician come from the same source: his capacity to voice the hopes and fears of people around him. But he sees his role realistically. "Occasionally," he writes, "I have the desire to cry out: 'I'm tired of playing the builder's role, I just want to do what every writer should do, to tell the truth!' ... Or: 'Take your own risks; I'm not your savior!' But I always bite my tongue before I speak, and remind myself of what Patočka once told me: the real test of a man is not how well he plays the role he has invented for himself, but how well he plays the role that destiny assigned to him."

Last fall, I went back to Eastern Europe. After having lived in Czechoslovakia for ten years, I was expelled in 1977 during the campaign the regime waged against Charter 77 and was only able to return to Prague on November 27 when the "revolution" was in its tenth day. I had already corresponded with Havel about the possibility of his adding some material to this book, to bring it up to date, but he had demurred on the grounds that the book was already finished. He had neither the time, he said, nor the inclination to add anything to it. But now that he was in the middle of this revolution, and playing such a central role in it, the idea of an update seemed more attractive than ever, and I hoped I might be able to persuade him to answer some supplementary questions.

In the frantic swirl of revolutionary events, Havel seemed as elusive as the wind. He was everywhere, but always on his way to somewhere else. I caught glimpses of him—once in the Theatre on the Balustrade, another time being swept from one meeting to another by his suite of volunteer bodyguards and handlers. Everyone had stories of "sightings." One of my friends was on Wenceslas Square the day Alexander Dubček first appeared on the balcony with Havel. When the demonstration was over and the spotlights were turned off, she saw Havel and Dubček, backlit against the window of the Melantrich building, doing a little dance.

Olga Havlová, and Václav's brother, Ivan, were helpful, but they could only suggest places to waylay him. Late one evening I was in the foyer of the divided flat he shares with Ivan when Havel came in. We greeted each other, and while the ubiquitous cameraman captured our encounter on video-tape, Havel graciously suggested a late supper some day in his favorite restaurant. But his keeper of the appointment book declared that this was impossible.

On December 7, I went to a press conference Havel gave in the Magic Lantern Theatre to pacify all the journalists who had been trying unsuccessfully to meet him. For the better part of an hour, he deflected questions about whether he intended to run for president. When an English journalist asked him what political lessons he had learned from his twelve years in Charter 77, Havel seemed relieved. "I'd have to think about it," he replied. "But there's one lesson I could mention right now. When a person tries to act in accordance with his conscience, when he tries to speak the truth, when he tries to behave like a citizen, even in conditions where citizenship is degraded, it won't necessarily lead anywhere, but it might. There's one thing, however, that will never lead anywhere, and that is speculating that such behavior will lead some-where."

I finally got to see Havel the day before I left Prague. By this time he had already made public his intention to run for president, with Alexander Dubček "at his side," and the streets of Prague were plastered with posters saying "Havel na Hrad"—Havel to the Castle. It was a gloomy, mid-December Sunday and Havel had ordered four hours of free family time, part of which was to be devoted to a walk in the park with Olga. We went into Ivan's living room which, like Havel's study next door, has a wonderful view of the Prague Castle, and talked about the book. He was still firm about considering it finished and not wanting to add any more. "The book has its own architecture, its own structure, and if we were to start adding material for every new edition, it would just keep rising like some strange loaf of Christmas bread," he said.

Then Olga called him to breakfast and he invited me to join him. As he ate his soup he talked, spinning off general impressions, ruminating on what was going on around him. "Revolution is chaos and confusion," he said, "and I'm a lover of order. I've always been put off by revolutions. I thought of them as natural disasters, the kind of thing that probably has to occur once in a while in history, but it's not the kind of thing you can plan for, or get ready for, or look forward to. And here I am, not only in a revolution, but right in the middle of it."

The phone rang and Olga came in to say that Dubček wanted to talk to him. "There goes another hour of my free time," said Havel to the ceiling. "Are you getting ready for our walk in the park?"

"Yes, but it's raining," Olga replied.

"Well, take an umbrella then," said Havel. "I've spent the last three weeks in basement rooms. I've got to get some air."

"I'm not sure we have an umbrella," said Olga.

"Then we'll buy one," said the future president. "No, wait a minute, it's Sunday; the stores are closed." Pause. "Ah, but it's almost Christmas; some of the stores will be open."

"Why buy an umbrella?" said Olga. "That's silly. We'll borrow one from Ivan."

That problem solved, Havel got up from the table, said goodbye, wished me luck, and shuffled off to talk to Dubček.

Here, then, is the book as Havel—President Havel—wanted it to be.

Paul Wilson
Toronto, March 1990

I

Growing Up "Outside"

You come from a well-known bourgeois family, as they say here. Today, with your fiftieth birthday on the horizon, how do you recall your childhood?

Yes, I do come from a bourgeois family, you might even say from a grand-bourgeois family. First the facts: My great-great-grandfather on my father's side was an important miller in Prague, but he had nine daughters and he frittered away his estate in dowries, so there was nothing left for my great-grandfather, his only son. My great-grandfather became a weigh-master, a position that was probably part blue-collar and part white-collar, which meant, if my guess is right, that he plunged from the heights of the middle class into the depths of the proletariat.

His son, my paternal grandfather, worked his way back up again; he studied architecture, borrowed some money, successfully paved a town square, and thus became a contractor. Then he built various things, pretty fin-de-siècle apartment buildings in Prague, but his main achievement was erecting the Lucerna Palace, the first steel-and-concrete building in Prague. He single-handedly did work that would require dozens of people today: he drew up the plans, made all the necessary calculations, supervised work on the construction site, looked after the financial side of things, and I don't know what else. He belonged to that first generation of genuine capitalists or bourgeoisie, the generation of self-made men who founded family firms, who began with nothing and achieved a lot. It's to him that we owe our bourgeois origins;

3

he was the one who first thrust our family into the ranks of the "bourgeoisie."

My father continued his work. He bought a vacant hillside south of Prague and built a subdivision of villas on it called Barrandov. He also constructed a terraced restaurant which, together with Lucerna, became the Lucerna and Barrandov Restaurant Enterprises. My uncle, my father's brother, had been involved in films ever since his youth, and he built film studios at Barrandov and became the biggest "film magnate" in the First Republic, and also during the Nazi protectorate.

It's hard for me to judge the extent to which my mother's family was bourgeois as well. Her father, Hugo Vavřečka, came from a poor family in Silesia, but he was a jack-of-all-trades: he was the national financial editor of *Lidové Noviny;* the Czechoslovak ambassador to various countries (he was even a government minister for a couple of days); he was manager of one of Baťa's factories; he was an occasional writer. For example, he wrote *Lelíčka,* which later became famous in the film version, starring Vlasta Burian. If you're interested in details about our family, you can read them in the six-part memoir by my father, which was published in samizdat. In the late sixties my brother and my wife and I prevailed upon my father to write his memoirs. Our original motives were "therapeutic": we knew that if he was going to live on and be mentally fit he had to have something to do. So we put him to work when he was almost eighty years old. The result was, I think, a remarkable and instructive book (Eva Kantůrková has written a very nice essay about it). You can feel in almost every sentence that what drove my father (as it had my grandfather) was not the notorious capitalistic longing for profit and surplus value, but enterprise, pure and simple—the will to create something. (My father, by the way, went into debt for the rest of his life over the construction of Barrandov, and he couldn't have been much of a millionaire, since he was not liable for the famous "millionaire's tax" after the war.) There's something almost touching about the way he apologizes at great length to the world for the fact that during the era of private enterprise there was nothing else he could do but carry on his enterprise privately. But, without going into too much detail, my father was a wonderful, kind man, despite being a capitalist and a bourgeois.

This, of course, does not mean at all that as a bourgeois child I simply accepted our bourgeois status, and capitalism as such, with no further reflection on the matter. It was much more complicated than that. During my childhood, especially when we lived at our country estate and I went to a village school, I enjoyed a great many advantages and perks. Unlike my fellow pupils and friends, I was a gentleman's son. Our family employed, as the custom was, domestics. I had a governess; we had a cook, a maid, a gardener, and a chauffeur. All of that put, between myself and those around me (I mean my poorer fellow students and our staff), a social barrier which, although I was still just a little guy, I was very much aware of and found hard to deal with. I understood it clearly as a handicap. I was ashamed of my advantages, my perks; I pleaded to be relieved of them and I longed for equality with others, not because I was some kind of childhood social revolutionary, but simply because I felt separate and excluded, because I felt around me a certain mistrust, a certain distance (I would hardly dare to call it class hatred), because I knew that between me and those around me there was an invisible wall, and because behind that wall—and this may seem paradoxical—I felt alone, inferior, lost, ridiculed. It was as though I subconsciously felt, or feared, that everyone had—rightly—entered into some kind of conspiracy against me, or at least some kind of silent mutual agreement that my privileges were undeserved, and that I, as the small possessor of these privileges, was ridiculous. In short, I felt "outside," excluded, humbled by my "higher" status. Add to that the fact that I was overweight and that the other children, as children will, laughed at my tubbiness, all the more so because it was an easy way to exact a kind of unconscious social revenge.

I wrote about this in one of my letters from prison, and tried to suggest how it influenced me. Today I believe this childhood experience influenced my entire future life, including my writing. My childhood feeling of exclusion, or of the instability of my place in the world (later, after the victory of communism, it was augmented by the experience of being the constant target of the "class struggle," which once more evoked the experience of exclusion through no fault of my own), could not but have an influence on the way I viewed the world—a view which is in fact a key to my plays. It is a view "from below," a view from the "outside," a view that has grown out of the experience of absurdity. What else but a profound feeling of being excluded can enable a person better to see the absurdity of the world and his own existence or, to put it more soberly, the absurd dimensions of the world and his own existence? My plays have been described as a Czech version of the theatre of the absurd. It's not up to me to decide to what extent I learned from or was instructed by absurd theatre as an artistic trend (probably quite a bit, even though I think that Kafka had a greater impact); still, I would scarcely have been so alive to the absurd outlines of the world without those early existential experiences I've mentioned here. So, in fact, I should be thankful for my bourgeois origins: obviously the feeling of being excluded through no fault of my own, both in childhood and later, when I was actively persecuted, turned out in the end to be productive. Sometimes I even wonder whether the original reason I began writing, or why I try to do anything at all, was simply to overcome this fundamental experience of not belonging, of embarrassment, of fitting in nowhere, of absurdity—or, rather, to learn how to live with it.

Naturally I don't blame or criticize my parents; they were good people who were only concerned for my own well-being, and they were locked into the social customs of their time, though no more or less than everyone is. I wouldn't even have held it against them if their unwittingly handicapping care for me had not ultimately turned into something in my favor. I benefited from the family setting in a very direct way. I grew up in the intellectual atmosphere of Masarykian humanism (my father was friends with Rádl, Ferdinand Peroutka, J. L. Fischer, Eduard Bass, etc.): I was surrounded by good books. Intellectually I got off to a good start. In puberty, as is often the case, I went through a period of revolting against my parents. Though I was never intellectually involved with communism (I have always been clear about that, even though I can't take all the credit for this), I have been, in my time, aggressively antibourgeois and no doubt I hurt my parents quite a bit (fortunately only in stupid talk), precisely during what was their worst period (in the 1950s). But that soon passed. Even so, something of that early self-awareness probably stayed with me: my bourgeois background—and this may seem odd, and you don't have to believe it if you don't want to—awakened (or, more exactly, strengthened) within me something like a social emotion, an antagonism toward undeserved privileges, toward unjust social barriers, toward any kind of so-called higher standing predetermined by birth or by anything else, toward any humiliation of human dignity. I think that everyone, as far as possible, should have the same chances. What use we make of them—that of course is another matter.

When you think about your origins in this way, aren't you attributing some validity to the rules of the system that has held sway in Czechoslovakia since 1948? My wife comes from a similar background: her family built a chain of department stores around Czechoslovakia; they built the White Swan, the first modern department store in Prague. To me it seems like a wonderful thing to have been born into a family that built something and was rich. Isn't it high time that we acknowledge these things?

I'm not sure whether my reflections on my bourgeois origins betray that I attribute some validity to the rules of the system. That is how I experienced them and that is how I see them, and I can't experience and see them in any other way, and I couldn't care less whether this is some form of concession to the ruling system or not. And anyway, no one ever develops and achieves self-awareness in a vacuum, beyond all eras and systems. The period you grow up in and mature in always influences your thinking. This in itself requires no self-criticism. What is more important is how you have allowed yourself to be influenced, whether by good or by evil.

I agree, but that's exactly why I'd like to come back to that question for a moment. Doesn't it seem to you that, after everything that's happened, we should try, once and for all, to reject these social heresies about socialism and equality?

You're obviously trying to get me to talk about my political opinions. I've never taken a systematic interest in politics, political science, or economics; I've never had a clear-cut political position, much less expressed it in public. I'm a writer, and I've always understood my mission to be to speak the truth about the world I live in, to bear witness to its terrors and its miseries—in other words, to warn rather than hand out prescriptions for change. Suggesting something better and putting it into practice is a politician's job, and I've never been a politician and never wanted to be. Even as a playwright, I've always believed that each member of the audience must sort the play out himself, because this is the only way his experience of it can be authentic; my job is not to offer him something ready-made. It is true that I've always been interested in politics, but only as an observer and a critic, not as someone who actually does it. (I'm ignoring the obvious truth, which is irrelevant in this context, that criticism of politics is a form of politics as well.)

Yet surely you have political opinions.

I've always had a fundamental though somewhat hazy notion of how social affairs should be organized, but I've never revealed it in any coherent fashion. For example, I've always been in favor of democracy, and for a long time I considered myself a socialist; I even called myself one ten years ago, in a conversation with Jiří Lederer. But I must add that this was the last time I ever used that word to define my political convictions, not because I subsequently underwent a radical change of opinion, or because I had converted from one thing to something else, but simply because I realized that the word no longer meant anything at all and that the use of it would obscure rather than illuminate my views. What is socialism anyway? Here, where you read about socialist railways, socialist business, socialist trade, socialist mothers, and socialist poetry, the word means nothing except loyalty to the government. But even in places where the word still means something, it can still mean so many different things!

My rejection of the word "socialism" derived from my traditional antipathy to overly fixed (and therefore semantically empty) categories, empty ideological phrases and incantations that petrify thought in a hermetic structure of static concepts—the more hermetic, the further they are from life. In my essays I've occasionally used concepts that I've invented, such as "the post-totalitarian system," or "antipolitical politics," but those were only occasional categories, chosen for a particular purpose, for a single essay, to be used in a certain context or atmosphere; I never felt compelled to return to them or use them again. They were meant to be situational linguistic aids, not binding categories. In short: I stopped calling myself a socialist without changing my political opinions. And, for that matter, even when I was still calling myself a socialist, I never identified with a particular political or economic doctrine, theory, or ideology, or with some project for improving the organization of the world. For me, socialism was more a human, moral, and emotional category. I was a socialist somewhat the way Peroutka and Černý were; they called themselves socialists as well. After all, there have been periods in history when everyone called himself a socialist who was on the side of the oppressed and the humiliated (that is, not on the side of the rulers), everyone who opposed undeserved advantages, inherited privileges, sponging on the powerless, of social injustices and the immoral barriers that degraded man and condemned him to the status of one who serves. I too was such an "emotional" and "moral" socialist, and I am still today, the only difference being that I no longer use that word to describe my position.

How would you describe your present ideas regarding a more meaningful way of organizing the world?

I have a better idea of this now than I had before, and certainly than I had when I was young, but my present notion is still extremely uncertain, vague, open to modification by new knowledge. In the first place, I think that the reasons for the crisis in which the world now finds itself are lodged in something deeper than a particular way of organizing the economy or a particular political system. The West and the East, though different in so many ways, are going through a single, common crisis. Reflecting on that crisis should be the starting point for every attempt to think through a better alternative. Where does the cause of this crisis lie? Václav Bělohradský puts it very nicely when he writes about this late period as one of conflict between an impersonal, anonymous, irresponsible, and uncontrollable juggernaut of power (the power of "megamachinery"), and the elemental and original interests of man as a concrete individual.

I too feel that somewhere here there is a basic tension out of which the present global crisis has grown. At the same time, I'm persuaded that this conflict—and the increasingly hypertrophic impersonal power itself—is directly related to the spiritual condition of modern civilization. This condition is characterized by loss: the loss of metaphysical certainties, of an experience of the transcendental, of any superpersonal moral authority, and of any kind of higher horizon. It is strange but ultimately quite logical: as soon as man began considering himself the source of the highest meaning in the world and the measure of everything, the world began to lose its human dimension, and man began to lose control of it.

We are going through a great departure from God which has no parallel in history. As far as I know, we are living in the middle of the first atheistic civilization. This departure has its own complex intellectual and cultural causes: it is related to the development of science, technology, and human knowledge, and to the whole modern upsurge of interest in the human intellect and the human spirit. I feel that this arrogant anthropocentrism of modern man, who is convinced he can know everything and bring everything under his control, is somewhere in the background of the present crisis. It seems to me that if the world is to change for the better it must start with a change in human consciousness, in the very humanness of modern man.

Man must in some way come to his senses. He must extricate himself from this terrible involvement in both the obvious and the hidden mechanisms of totality, from consumption to repression, from advertising to manipulation through television. He must rebel against his role as a helpless cog in the gigantic and enormous machinery hurtling God knows where. He must discover again, within himself, a deeper sense of responsibility toward the world, which means responsibility toward something higher than himself. Modern science has realized this (though not the proprietors of "the scientific world view"), but it cannot find a remedy. The power to awaken this new responsibility is beyond its reach; such a thing can be resolved neither scientifically nor technically. It may seem like a paradox, but one I think will prove true, that only through directing ourselves toward the moral and the spiritual, based on respect for some "extramundane" authority—for the order of nature or the universe, for a moral order and its superpersonal origin, for the absolute—can we arrive at a state in which life on this earth is no longer threatened by some form of "megasuicide" and becomes bearable, has, in other words, a genuinely human dimension. This direction, and this direction alone, can lead to the creation of social structures in which a person can once more be a person, a specific human personality.

Does this mean you refuse to take a position on systemic problems, and instead suggest that mankind wait for a moral and spiritual revival before tackling a solution?

In the first place: As I understand it, spiritual renewal (I once called it an "existential revolution") is not something that one day will drop out of heaven into our laps, or be ushered in by a new messiah. It is a task that confronts us all, every moment of our existence. We all can and must "do something about it," and we can do it here and now. No one else can do it for us, and therefore we can't wait for anyone else. I could point to a great deal of evidence to show that this is already going on. Aren't there a lot of people in the world who aren't apathetic yet and are trying to "do something about it"? That's the first thing.

The second thing: Whatever transformations or shifts take place in the intellectual and moral sphere are not happening somewhere outside or above the world, in some kind of other world, but here and now, on the terrain of our social life. They're only visible, we only know about them at all, because of their social impact. They "take place" through social life and in it, somewhat the way a sculptor's idea "takes place" in the material he uses. Therefore it's not true that you should first think up an idea for a better world and only then "put it into practice," but, rather, through the fact of your existence in the world, you create the idea or manifest it—create it, as it were, from the "material of the world," articulate it in the "language of the world."

So you do have a more concrete notion of a better social system after all?

I've already admitted to having one. The traditional political debate between the right and the left revolves around the ownership of the means of production, to put it in Marxist terms: that is, around the question of whether business enterprises should be privately run or made public property. Frankly, I don't see that that is the main problem. I would put it this way: The most important thing is that man should be the measure of all structures, including economic structures, and not that man be made to measure for those structures. The most important thing is not to lose sight of personal relationships—i.e., the relationships between man and his co-workers, between subordinates and their superiors, between man and his work, between this work and its consequences, and so on.

An economy that is totally nationalized and centralized (i.e., run by the command system), such as we're familiar with in our country, has a catastrophic effect on all such relationships. An ever-deepening chasm opens up between man and the economic system, which is why this type of economy works so badly. Having lost his personal relationship to his work, his company, to the many decisions about the substance and the purpose of his work and its consequences, he loses interest in the work itself. The company allegedly belongs to everyone, but in reality it belongs to no one. A worker's activity is dissipated in the anonymous, automatic functioning of the system, for which no one is responsible and which no one understands. All the natural motive forces of economic life, such as human inventiveness and enterprise, just payment for work done, market relations, competition, and so on, are scrapped. No one is properly paid, or properly punished, for the results of his work. People lose—and this is the worst of all—any contact whatsoever with the meaning of their work. Everything falls into the enormous pit of impersonal, anonymous, automatic economic functioning, from work done by the least hired hand right up to decisions made by the bureaucrats in the office of central planning.

All this is notoriously familiar. At the same time, I don't believe that we can wave a magic wand and dispose of these problems by a change of ownership, or that all we need do to remedy the situation is bring back capitalism. The point is that capitalism, albeit on another level and not in such trivial forms, is struggling with the same problems (alienation, after all, was first described under capitalism): it is well known, for instance, that enormous private multinational corporations are curiously like socialist states; with industrialization, centralization, specialization, monopolization, and finally with automation and computerization, the elements of depersonalization and the loss of meaning in work become more and more profound everywhere. Along with that goes the general manipulation of people's lives by the system (no matter how inconspicuous such manipulation may be, compared with that of the totalitarian state). IBM certainly works better than the Škoda plant, but that doesn't alter the fact that both companies have long since lost their human dimension and have turned man into a little cog in their machinery, utterly separated from what, and for whom, that machinery is working, and what the impact of its product is on the world. I would even say that, from a certain point of view, IBM is worse than Škoda. Whereas Škoda merely grinds out the occasional obsolete nuclear reactor to meet the needs of backward COMECON members, IBM is flooding the world with ever more advanced computers, while its employees have no influence over what their product does to the human soul and to human society. They have no say in whether it enslaves or liberates mankind, whether it will save us from the apocalypse or simply bring the apocalypse closer. Such "megamachinery" is not constructed to the measure of man, and the fact that IBM is capitalist, profit-oriented, and efficient while Škoda is socialist, money-losing, and inefficient, seems secondary to me.

Perhaps it is clearer now what kind of "systemic notions" I favor. The most important thing today is for economic units to maintain—or, rather, renew—their relationship with individuals, so that the work those people perform has human substance and meaning, so that people can see into how the enterprise they work for works, have a say in that, and assume responsibility for it. Such enterprises must have—I repeat—a human dimension; people must be able to work in them as people, as beings with a soul and a sense of responsibility, not as robots, regardless of how primitive or highly intelligent they may be. It isn't easy to find an economic expression of this indicator, but I think it's more important than all the other economic indicators we've managed to isolate so far.

But it's not just man as worker that we're concerned about; it's the general meaning of his work. And to my mind the criterion for that should be, again, the human quality of that work in the broadest sense of the word, not just production quantity, or an abstract "quality *per se.*" Again, this is hard to express in whatever bell curve of economic growth you choose, capitalist or socialist. For example, it's important that man have a home on this earth, not just a dwelling place; it's important that his world have an order, a culture, a style; it's important that the landscape be respected and cultivated with sensitivity, even at the expense of growth in productivity; it's important that the secret inventiveness of nature, its infinite variety, the inscrutable complexity of its interconnections, be honored; it's important that cities and streets have their own face, their own atmosphere, their own style; it's important that human life not be reduced to stereotypes of production and consumption, but that it be open to all possibilities; it's important that people not be a herd, manipulated and standardized by the choice of consumer goods and consumer television culture, whether this culture is offered to him by three giant competing capitalist networks or a single giant noncompetitive socialist network. It is important, in short, that the superficial variety of one system, or the repulsive grayness of the other, not hide the same deep emptiness of life devoid of meaning.

Given this, I would tend to favor an economic system based on the maximum possible plurality of many decentralized, structurally varied, and preferably small enterprises that respect the specific nature of different localities and different traditions and that resist the pressures of uniformity by maintaining a plurality of modes of ownership and economic decision-making, from private (indispensable in the area of crafts, trades, services, small business, and retail enterprises and areas of agriculture and, of course, in culture as well) through various types of cooperative and shareholding ventures, collective ownerships (connected with self-management schemes), right up to state ownership. Nothing in this, of course, should be allowed, in its own area, to preclude the genesis of anything different. Any eventual central regulation of this variegated economic scene (and some degree of minimal regulation is essential) should be based on nothing more than a highly evolved sensitivity to what contributes to the general good of the human being, and what, on the contrary, limits and destroys it. The referee in such matters, of course, could not be a state bureaucracy but a democratically elected political body that relies on a continuing dialogue between public opinion and expert opinion.

As for the political system, I would not depend too heavily on the traditional approach, with two or three large political parties, as the only possible guarantee of democracy. If all power in the communist countries is in the hands of a bureaucratic apparatus run by a single political party, then this, understandably, is worse than if there are two parties, both of which are held in check by freely expressed public opinion, and between which the public can choose in elections. But that's not ideal either. It would seem to make more sense if, again, people rather than political parties were elected (that is, if people could be elected without party affiliation). Politicians would solicit the support of the electors as individuals in their own right, not merely as appendages to the mega-machinery of parties or as party favorites. There should be no limit to the number of political parties, but they should, rather, be something like political clubs, where people could refine their opinions, get to know each other personally, and seek to determine who among them would be the best to administer the affairs of the *polis*. Parties should not take direct part in elections, nor should they be allowed to give anyone, *a priori*, the crutches of power. In other words, they should not participate directly in power, since when they do they inevitably become bureaucratic, corrupt, and undemocratic. They should instead provide those who participate in power—having been elected—with an intellectual base, with ideas, with opportunities to hone their opinions.

I'm not against solidarity and cohesiveness among a wide variety of interest groups and associations that share common views. I'm only against anything that obscures personal responsibility or gives anyone perks as a reward for obedience to a group that is aiming to take power.

That is my personal "utopia." I don't like talking about it, and you've been the first to force me to put it into words. I hope that even these brief, hesitant remarks will confirm my notion that a genuinely fundamental and hopeful improvement in "systems" cannot happen without a significant shift in human consciousness, and that it cannot be accomplished through a simple organizational trick. It's hard to imagine the kind of system I've tried to describe here coming about unless man, as I've said, "comes to his senses." This is something no revolutionary or reformer can bring about; it can be only the natural expression of a more general state of mind, the state of mind in which man can see beyond the tip of his own nose and prove capable of taking on—under the aspect of eternity—responsibility even for the things that don't immediately concern him, and relinquish something of his private interest in favor of the interest of the community, the general interest. Without such a mentality, even the most carefully considered project aimed at altering systems will be for naught.

Do you think that any essential change in perception, thought, the hierarchy of values, and so on is possible at all without a war, or some kind of ecological catastrophe?

I don't think catastrophes are essential for all improvements in human thought, nor do I think they automatically produce such changes.

You mentioned that your father was friends with the writer Eduard Bass, the journalist Ferdinand Peroutka, the philosopher J. L. Fischer, and others like them. What kind of memories do you have of these people?

I consider it most important of all that from very early childhood I had books by these authors at my disposal. When I was ten years old, I read Peroutka's *Today;* I read Čapek and Masaryk. We had them all at home, and it was a natural intellectual background, something I took for granted. In my youth, of course, I couldn't have met many of these people; they'd either died or emigrated. When I was still very young, I used to be in frequent contact with J. L. Fischer, a rather remarkable philosopher and the creator of "structural philosophy," a structuralistic variation on democratic socialism which tried to oppose Marxism with a system that was more open, more dynamic, and more democratic. I have fond memories of Fischer; he was the first one to raise some philosophical questions with me and draw my attention to important books of philosophy. But the very first Czech philosopher to have some influence on me was Josef Šafařík, a reclusive philosopher from Brno. Thanks to my grandfather, I had known him since my childhood and his book *Seven Letters to Melin* was my personal philosophical bible in my early youth. I am still friends with Šafařík, and recently he sent me a manuscript of what is probably his cardinal work, *On the Way to the Last.*

Concerning people you asked about, when I was very young I was friends with Edvard Valenta, and at his place I first met Václav Cerný, Olga Scheinpflugová, and Pavel Eisner. It wasn't until many years later, in America and Western Europe, that I met many important personalities of prewar Czechoslovakia and of the period immediately after the Second World War. In 1968 I traveled a great deal and spent much of my time visiting exiles, because the phenomenon of exiles fascinated me. I was working on a book on exile, and I looked up about thirty important personalities in the post–February 1948 wave of exiles, from people like Zenkel, Lettrich, Slavík, Majer, and other politicians, to Peroutka, Ducháček, and Tigrid, and even Voskovec (in fact, I stayed at his place in New York for several weeks).

I asked all of them the same question: Under what circumstances would you be willing to return to Czechoslovakia? It didn't sound nearly as absurd then as it does today. Most of them gave me lengthy, reflective answers, which I then combined with my own impressions, insights, and thoughts on the theme of exile. It was to have been serialized in *Literární Noviny,* on the last page, where long pieces of reportage and essays appeared, but it never happened: my book was beaten out by the Soviet occupation. Later, in a critical moment, I destroyed the entire file, so that today it exists only in the archives of the Ministry of the Interior, which had, as I later discovered, managed to photograph the entire manuscript.

I should add that in the 1960s I had a somewhat different attitude toward exile from that of most of those who were publicly active then. Reform communists still saw those post-February exiles as their former political opponents, and they would have considered it supremely bad tactics (since it could have been misused by the regime) to give any thought to exile at all. For them, exile was taboo. Of course, it was also taboo for noncommunists, who for the most part assumed that, if the communists couldn't afford to risk something, so much the less could they. At the time, any contact whatsoever with exiles was perceived as extremely dangerous, indefensible, even suicidal, so there was no open communication between the domestic scene and the exiles. Of course, *Svědectví* had for some time been publishing texts from home as well; Tigrid had his own collaborators inside Czechoslovakia, but that was secret, and had to be kept that way.

In this connection, I remember the trial in 1967 of the writer Jan Beneš, who was sentenced to a term in prison for having sent some texts to Tigrid. I know something about it, partly because I was interrogated in the matter, and partly because I tried to help Beneš inside the Writers' Union. I remember how difficult it was; no one wanted to burn his own fingers, and nothing happened until the eve of the famous Fourth Writers' Union Congress, when Jan Procházka read my appeal for Beneš in a plenary session of the party caucus. I didn't like that ostrichlike attitude to the exile, and it seemed especially absurd in 1968, when there was an alleged attempt in our country to create a combination of democracy and socialism, which was precisely what the parties in the National Front had tried to achieve twenty years before. That was why I tried to open the question of exile. But I see I've got away from your original question.

Let's return to it, then. You met with Ferdinand Peroutka. He was our most effective journalist between the two wars. What impression did he make on you?

In America, I met Peroutka several times. I was his guest in his cottage on Lost Lake, and I recorded a conversation with him that went on for several hours. God knows in which basement of the Czechoslovak Radio it finally ended up. Understandably, I found it an enormously valuable and interesting conversation. Peroutka, very deliberately, matter-of-factly, and with surprising insight, analyzed the situation in our country (this was 1968), and what I remember most vividly is an idea that I've only come to appreciate with the passage of time. He said that, no matter how things turned out here— and in such matters he tended to be skeptical—the most important of all would be to preserve from the Prague Spring the less remarkable but, from the point of view of the future, the immensely significant thing: the plurality of social association from below. Even on the lowest and least political level, this tendency gave a certain institutional form to a variety of interests, opinions, destinies, lives, points of view, feelings; it was also a political expression of the genuine intentions of life, and an instrument to defend life against the totalitarian demands of the system. Peroutka considered the relentless defiance of those small social units to be more important for the future than all those sensational political revelations of the Prague Spring. Today I can see how farsighted he was: the renewal process did not provide enough time for this field to develop the unmappable variety and complexity necessary to put it beyond the reach of manipulation and to reflect the real potential of society, which was precisely why everything could be so quickly and so drastically suppressed! In fact, it's only now, many years later and in incomparably more difficult conditions, that various focuses and cells of relatively independent life are beginning to revitalize society.

On the other hand, of course, there were matters in which Peroutka and I did not see eye to eye. He belonged more to the Central Europe of the twenties and thirties than to the America of the sixties. He didn't feel at home there; he didn't understand America, as he admitted himself, and he didn't like it very much. His views of American affairs were too right-wing and conservative for my taste. For example, he believed every word of the Warren Commission report on Kennedy's death. He had no understanding for the hippie movement or for the tempestuous era of the sixties, with its music, its protests, its visual art, and all the rest of it. I felt he was no longer capable of analyzing any of it, and that he thought of it all as an incomprehensible anomaly. When he saw bare-footed boys and girls walking around New York with chains around their necks like some aboriginal Christians, he interpreted it as a sad expression of moral degeneration which should probably have been suppressed. Of course, it had to do with his age as well: he was well over seventy, whereas I belonged to the generation of the Beatles.

I'd like to go back a little bit, to your biography—

In 1948 they confiscated all our family property and we became objects of the class struggle. My father, it must be said, was so well liked in Lucerna that even after nationalization he was hired as an adviser to the national administrator and planner. For years we would go to Lucerna for lunch every Sunday, and the administrator would sit with us. His relationship to our family was almost intimate and conspiratorial. Former employees would prepare special dishes for us, wink at us, and serve us enormous portions. It was a pure example of class reconciliation, within the firm, of course. Perhaps too my father had been allowed to work there because before the war he had rented the grand Lucerna ballroom to the Communist Party for its congresses, and some rather untypically sentimental functionary may have remembered that.

Otherwise we were not spared. We became victims of "Action B," in which the bourgeoisie were forced to move out of Prague. We were assigned to some tiny hamlet in the border regions where there was no chance of adequate employment or accommodations. It was intended to be a kind of exile, but through some complicated official machinations we eventually managed not to be moved out; we clung, with typical bourgeois tenacity, to two little rooms in the very flat where we had lived to that time. Action B later ran out of steam, and we began gradually to make ourselves at home in that flat, where our family still lives today. For my brother, Ivan, and me, of course, the class struggle meant above all that we couldn't continue our education. In 1951 I finished elementary school and went right to work; it was impossible for someone in my social position to get into high school. I was assigned to apprentice as a carpenter, but my family was worried: I get dizzy easily and they were justifiably afraid that I might fall off a roof. Through various connections, they got me a position as a laboratory assistant, which I somewhat regretted later: had I become a carpenter, at least I would have a skill.

I was a laboratory assistant for five years. But, thanks to the fact that things were still disorganized, something happened that could not have happened two years later: immediately after starting work in the lab, I enrolled in night school, where I managed to complete my matriculation. By way of explanation, the night school had been established for working-class managers to broaden their education, not for bourgeois children who did not make it into full-time day school. The level of teaching was, of course, very low. To this day I cannot understand how I managed to do everything I did: I spent eight hours at work; I had to travel right across Prague to get to work; I sometimes had to work night shifts; I spent four hours a day at night school; I was exhausted from work and school, and yet I managed to attend a slew of dancing courses and balls, read a lot of books, dig around in secondhand bookstores, visit various writers, carry on endless debates with my friends, and write my own texts!

If my calculations are correct, you began writing in 1952, a year after you finished elementary school—

Earlier. In fact, I'd been writing ever since they taught me the alphabet. I wrote poems, serials, and when I was thirteen I even wrote a philosophical book. When I was a laboratory technician I couldn't help myself and wrote a popular brochure on the structure of the atom, and I constructed a hitherto nonexistent three-dimensional model of the periodic table of the elements. When I was fifteen I began to write poetry more consistently, and felt drawn more clearly to the humanities.

At that time, I also found myself in a certain intellectual circle—I may even have been one of the founders—made up of friends of various backgrounds: from the evening high school, from secondary school, and from primary school. We called ourselves the Thirty-sixers, since all of us had been born in 1936. It lasted from 1951 to about 1953. We published a typewritten magazine, we held symposia, and we even held congresses. The Thirty-sixers were divided into sections (I recall, for example, that we had a literary and a political-economic section) where we had our first youthful debates. When I think back on it, my hair stands on end: if we'd been five years older, we'd have almost certainly ended up in Mirov; in those days, you could easily get twenty years for that kind of thing.

I kept on writing poetry until I was called up for the army; I wrote several collections, which were fortunately never published. Although I was already, in effect, being persecuted, I still have fond memories of that period; it was the time of my first excited quests, discovering things of value that were hidden from view, discovering myself. The same signs and banners that are there today were in all the streets; the same books by the same people, Pujmanová and Fučík and so on, were in all the libraries; and there was no evidence anywhere that another culture, different from the socialist-realist one which was enjoying such enormous official support, existed. So it was all the more adventurous for an eager young man searching for the "second culture."

But to be more concrete: A friend of my father's at the time arranged an audience with Jaroslav Seifert. I brought him my first poetic efforts, and to this day I still have, somewhere, a nice letter that he wrote to me about them afterward. I can't remember whether I was alone the first time I went to his place, or whether I went with my friends Jiří Kuběna and

Miloš Forman, but we certainly visited him a couple of times later in that combination (the three of us also visited Nezval; it was rather funny—Nezval received us between visits from two world peace delegations—but he was kind). At the time, however, I was already moving away from Seifert (every poetical generation after Devětsil had to go through its own youthful anti-Seifert rebellion) and so I once told him I loved Vladimír Holan, and his immediate response was that I should definitely go and see him, that he'd be glad of a visit. I was terrified by the notion that somewhere in Prague, living and available to me, was the physical person of this great poetical sorcerer. Seifert sent me to the Isle of Kampa, and from then on I visited Holan regularly, about once a month, always with a bottle of wine. I stopped probably sometime in 1956, because, among other things, his anti-Semitic talk bothered me. In human terms I don't think he was an anti-Semite, but he obviously thought he had somehow to justify his conversion to Catholicism by talking like that. (My friend Zdeněk Urbánek will undoubtedly object that anti-Semitism is all of a piece and that you can't separate it into "human" and "ideological" components. Of course you're right, Zdeněk, but please try to understand what I wanted to say through this awkward formulation.) Holan had an odd, almost demonic personality, yet I can still say that I was, to some extent, friends with him; I even celebrated his fiftieth birthday with him in Všenory; we got drunk on wine that had been sent to him, clearly out of a guilty conscience, by the Writers' Union.

During one visit to the Isle of Kampa (it may even have been the first visit, most probably with Kuběna and Forman, since I think I'd have been too shy to go there the first time alone), I met the poet Jan Zábrana, and we became close friends. He was older and more experienced than we were, and he told us about things we'd been unaware of until then, things we couldn't really have known—about Group 42 and Jiří Kolář and many other authors who weren't allowed to publish. Naturally, in various complex and roundabout ways, we immediately started looking for the relevant books and old magazines, and of course we fell in love with them at once. For us, Group 42 became the last living achievement of Czech poetry, perhaps of Czech art. We related completely to what they had done; those first collections of poetry by Kainar and Kolář, the essays by Chalupecký and others, had the authority of a compass. Naturally we longed to meet our new idols in person, and so once again we set out on the exciting quest for silenced artists. The very thought that these people were living among us somewhere and that we might meet them was fascinating. I remember, for example, how exciting it was when, sometime in the late fifties, I first saw Professor Jan Patočka, whose texts I had already hungrily devoured in the university library (you were not allowed to borrow them, but a librarian looked the other way). My first visit at Jiří Kolář's place is worth recalling. My friends and I used to meet every Saturday at noon in the Café Slavia. Once Viola Fischer and I (and, by the way, she was the daughter of J. L. Fischer) decided to visit Kolář. We found his telephone number, and Viola, who was braver than I was, called him. He said, "Sure, come around three on Saturday." We sat in the Café Slavia, waiting impatiently, until two-thirty; then we said goodbye to our friends and set out for Vršovice to meet Kolář. When we got there, the door was opened by a gentleman who two hours before had been sitting at the table beside us in the Café Slavia and whom we knew very well by sight (he was usually there with his friends Kamil Lhoták, Zdeněk Urbánek, Vladimír Fuka, Jan Rychlík, Josef Hiršal, and others). So the gentleman I'd been greeting for some time now as one regular to another was Kolář! He then showed us his books of *cyclages, confrontages* and some other things he was working on with Zdeněk Urbánek and others, which later led to his becoming a visual artist. From that time—and I can't remember whether it was 1952 or 1953—until the 1960s, various friends of my own age and I would sit with Kolář at his famous table in the Café Slavia. Later we even collaborated with him: for example, we organized, with Kolář's blessing, various semiofficial appearances in the Umělecká Beseda, or artist's club. We even participated in the samizdat of the time.

My closest literary companions and friends were Jiří Kuběna, Věra Linhartová, Josef Topol, Jan Zábrana, and other authors, who were roughly my own age, who had never published before, and who felt that the "second culture" of the time was their "natural world." With the presumption of youth, we also counted among ourselves some older and already mature writers who had not been able to publish anything yet either, like Josef Škvorecký and Bohumil Hrabal. These sessions in Kolář's circle opened up to me hitherto unknown horizons of modern art. But, most important of all, they were a kind of university of writers' morality, if I may put it in such august terms. Kolář was a distinctive preacher with a great understanding for young authors and for everything new, and he had a spontaneous interest, in his endearingly authoritative way (thanks to which his advice or his ideas often took the form of injunctions), in helping what was new into the world. He judged the moral and noetic dimensions of literature by his own, rather strict, standards; this is clear, for instance, in his *Master Sun,* an extensive collection of imperatives that poetry heaps upon the poet. And although later I began to write, independently of his literary influence, things that were utterly unlike what Kolář expected of me, these efforts of mine, both in literature and in the field of civic affairs, culture, and politics, would be unimaginable without his initial lesson in a writer's responsibility.

For me the 1950s was a very special time in which, quite naturally and of my own accord, I slipped into the company of those who were working on the borderline between what was permitted and not permitted, and more often than not beyond those borders. I felt at home among them long before I myself was cut off from public culture, and even long before I got into that public culture. Today I see many young authors who are just starting out, who are unencumbered and unstigmatized by any literary or political past, and who are therefore not on any index of forbidden authors. Theoretically there is nothing to prevent them from trying to climb the road to Parnassus—that is, from sending their works to exist-ing literary magazines, from trying to get published officially. Nevertheless, they deliberately choose samizdat. Their fun-damental feelings about life, their initial experience of the world, and their poetics were so at odds with everything official that they would understand publishing in official magazines and publishing houses almost as a betrayal of themselves.

I understand them because at their age I was in the same position: the world of official literature was alien to me, and of no interest; I ridiculed it. For me, it was a hundred times more important to participate in the activity symbolized by Kolář's table at the Café Slavia than it was to publish my work somewhere. I went to the Writers' Union club two or three times out of curiosity; they held occasional round-table dis-cussions or literary matinees for the public, but I must say I felt very out of place. Oddly enough, this feeling remained with me, and survived later developments: long after I be-came a member of the Writers' Union, long after I had sat on various committees and used the club in a working capacity, I still always felt miserable there. Which was true as well for the writers' château at Dobříš.

And yet Dobříš was the first place where you actually drew attention to yourself! I'm thinking of the meeting of young writers held in Dobříš in the autumn of 1956.

I have to preface this again with a short autobiographical introduction. In 1956 I was no longer a laboratory technician but a student. After graduating from night school in 1954, I applied to various arts faculties to study art history and phi-losophy, and to the film faculty of AMU (my "agent" on the admissions committee was Milan Kundera, who supported my application; I point this out because, thanks to our later public disagreements, many people think that we have always been professional and personal enemies, which is of course nonsense). But I was not accepted anywhere. Because of the large number of applicants for these faculties, political profile was an especially significant factor in the admissions procedures.

A year later, in 1955, after repeatedly unsuccessful attempts to study something I was really interested in, I became eligible for the draft. Obviously I didn't want to go into the army, and so, out of desperation (combined with ineptitude), I applied to the faculty of economics in the Czech University of Technology, where they were admitting anyone, and where I too was accepted, in the department of public transport. I had persuaded myself that economics would somehow bring me closer to the social sciences, but I was wrong. The courses did not interest me—we studied things like the nature of gravel and sand, and road construction—and after two years of this I decided to try to transfer to AMU. I can't recall now whether I applied for the film or the theatre faculty—probably film (I only applied for the film faculty once, and if it was in 1957, then this was when Kundera acted as my "agent")— but again I wasn't accepted. I couldn't go back to the technical university and didn't really want to, so I ended up in the army all the same and did my stint from 1957 to 1959.

But we're talking about 1956. At the time, something was beginning to change in the social climate. This was after the historic Twentieth Congress of the Communist Party of the Soviet Union, and after the famous Second Congress of the Writers' Union of Czechoslovakia, at which Seifert and František Hrubín had made courageous speeches. It was the period of the student Maytime festival, the *Majáles;* the first timid criticisms of the 1950 show trials were appearing; and so on. The sharp division between official and independent culture was becoming blurred, and there was hope that some of the books which had not been published would start coming out; the writers' congress began talking openly about writers who had been banished from literature, and even about those who'd been imprisoned.

If I'm not mistaken, it was a resolution passed at the Second Congress that founded *Květen* as a magazine for the young generation of writers. As far as I was concerned, this magazine was part of the official literary establishment (most of the contributors were communists), and it had to tip its hat to official ideology, and yet I also felt that the contributors were making some effort to abandon the rigid schemata of social realism and get closer to life itself. *Květen* promoted the notion of "a poetry of everyday life," according to which poetry was supposed to be open to daily human experience, the kind of experience that—as the authors in *Květen* dimly felt—was fatally absent in the official image of the world and of life. The combination of *Květen*'s intentions with its dependence on official ideology made the magazine oddly halfbaked, inconsistent, embarrassing, and aimless; for my taste, there was something hopelessly diffuse and awkward about it. Simply put, it was full of internal contradictions. But the times were changing now; these people were trying to do something, and they deserved more than ridicule. It seemed possible to start a dialogue with them, so I wrote a letter to the editor expressing my doubts; I pointed out the internal contradictions in the magazine and its program, and I asked why it did not reflect upon the heritage of Group 42, why they had no relationship to it and, indeed, seemed not even to know about it when, after all, it was Group 42 that had so marvelously opened poetry up to the modern city and the contradictions in modern life! To my astonishment, *Květen* published my letter. These people had all graduated from the Charles University in literature and clearly knew nothing whatever about Group 42, whose star had shone publicly only a few years before, but they were genuinely willing, to a certain extent, to engage in dialogue, and they were determined, however belatedly, to discover things that had been hidden from them in school. My letter provoked a discussion on the pages of *Květen,* and it was probably because of this, my first published text, that I found myself on a list of neophyte authors and was then officially invited to a three-day conference (or was it a political meeting?) of young writers in Dobříš. I went there with decidedly mixed feelings: On the one hand, I felt a slight antipathy to that whole milieu, and I asked myself what I was really doing there. On the other hand, as a complete unknown, I was uncomfortable at suddenly finding myself among such renowned people as Marie Majerová, Marie Pujmanová, Jan Drda, Pavel Kohout, and others; the place was literally swarming with them. Yet my rather irrational respect for famous people was strangely at odds with my antipathy toward them. Since they'd invited me and were putting me up for three days, I felt I had to take advantage of the situation and tell them plainly what I had against them; it would have been shameful to accept their invitation and then remain silent.

I prepared an extensive contribution in which I elaborated on everything I had so cautiously set out in my letter to *Květen,* knowing that my speech would not be subjected to any kind of censorship. I drew attention to the ambiguous relationship between official and suppressed literature; I accused them of being hypocritical when they called themselves reformers who wanted to "take a new look at old mistakes," to "correct blunders," to open the window to truth, and yet hesitated to go through with it and refused to listen to what they should logically be doing if they meant what they said.

From the outset, the atmosphere of the conference was strange and rather high-strung, since by sheer coincidence it was taking place while the Soviet army was putting down the Budapest uprising. Morever, it had clearly not been well prepared: there was no opening address and no program; someone from the presidium simply declared the conference open and asked if anyone had anything to say. The response was sepulchral silence—obviously no one had prepared anything. So I put my hand up. My contribution more or less determined the course of the conference. In one way or another, most of the discussions in the conference hall and in the corridors were about subjects that I had raised. It was a comic situation: here were a lot of famous authors with a lot of

published books to their credit, along with editors and journalists, all of them members of the party and the Writers'
Union, and their deliberations were determined by an entirely unknown person, a public-transport student who had
wandered in, God knows how. The reactions to my contribution were—and could not have been otherwise—wildly
contradictory: they argued with me, they criticized me, they
even defended me; at the same time, however, they called my
speech "daringly critical" and "courageous" and said that I
was one of those voices that had to be listened to in all seriousness at that time.

This confusion reflected something of the general confusion of that whole era: Stalin had fallen from grace; Hungary
was bleeding in revolution; in Poland, Gomulka had virtually
been brought straight out of jail and put on the throne; and
no one knew where it was all heading, what still applied and
what no longer did, and what one should think of it all. There
was even a possibility that Slánský, whose death by hanging
some of those present had publicly and with great pathos and
drama demanded only a few years before, might be rehabili-
tated. I remember Mrs. Pujmanová declaring her astonishment that I was talking about some forgotten poets while
socialism was fighting for its life in the streets of Budapest.
From the floor, I retorted that I didn't understand how they
could hold a costly conference on poetry when it was forbidden to talk about Czech poets. In the end, Jiří Hájek gave a
long-winded, dialectically balanced speech in which he praised
me faintly for starting a heated discussion and then put me
in my place by stressing that Czech literature would never
allow itself to be robbed of its partisan socialist nature. He
concluded by saying something to the effect that we all had
a lot to learn yet and that the most important thing was
creation.

My entry into public literary life, then, had a whiff of rebellion about it, and this has somehow clung to me: many still
consider me a controversial person, to this day. Not that I
welcome it: I am certainly not a revolutionary or a "rebellious

bohemian" (Jindrich Chalupecky's term); it just seems that, given the logic of things, I always manage to find myself, whether I want to or not, in such a position. As a matter of interest, many of those who thirty years ago debated with me excitedly far into the night and, as they got drunker, would alternately heap ashes on their own heads and accuse me of betraying socialism, have long since become my friends and sail together with me on the good ship *Samizdat*. I must say that they have gained my respect. Because I was used to being on the outside (in periods when I was publicly acknowledged or praised or rewarded, I always considered it an exception and a mistake), my exclusion from public life in the 1970s, did not catch me so much off balance. But these people had been spoiled and pampered by power from the very first lines they wrote. They had audiences with the president at twenty, they were decorated with state prizes for literature, they were used to the limelight, and when their fall into the abyss came, it must have been incomparably more difficult. Gradually, however, they have come to understand that it was not a fall at all, but an ascent—albeit one that cost them dearly— toward inner freedom, a freedom which, back then in Dobříš, they were far from possessing.

II

Writing for the Stage

*How did you become involved in theatre? What made you
decide to devote your life to it? Is it true that your wife was a
factor? You began, I understand, as a stagehand in the ABC
Theatre—*

As I've already said, I studied at the technical university
until 1957, then did my two years in the army. I served with
the sappers in České Budějovice and had rather a hard time
of it. They probably put me with the sappers because of my
social origins: our army borrowed from the Soviets the tradition of sending the less worthwhile elements of the population to serve with the sappers, because in any action the
sappers go in first and lose a higher percentage of men. There
were boys in our unit who had already been to prison, and
there were people who had been to university but had some
black marks in their book.

It was in the army that I first came into active contact with
theatre, and it happened under rather serious circumstances.
At that time, the army still strongly supported cultural activity; the regiments and the divisions used culture to gain
greater legitimacy, and they were judged by their performances. Along with my buddy and fellow soldier Carl Brynda
(today he's the head of drama in the State Theatre in Os-
trava), I founded a regimental theatre company. The first year
we put on Kohout's well-known play *September Nights;* I played
a negative character, First Lieutenant Škrovánek. Of course
we had a lot of fun doing it; the main reason we were doing
theatre in the first place was that it got us out of some of the
training and drill. I have several funny memories. Once the

commander of my company, after seeing our performance, called me into his tent and told me that I had played Škrovánek so convincingly that this amounted to a confession of who I really was. I tried in vain to explain to him that Lieutenant Škrovánek had ambitions to become company commander, whereas I had no such ambitions, since my only desire was to get through my hitch in the army with a minimum of fuss. He punished me in a way that I welcomed: he demoted me from *pancéřovník,* which he considered an honor, and in doing so he liberated me from the responsibility of dragging a bazooka, along with everything else I had to carry, to every drill, and cleaning it every Saturday.

My second year in the army, Brynda and I decided to do something that required a lot of bravado: we decided to write our own play. We thought that, if our battalion, and ultimately our division, could boast of an original play based on army life, our drama troupe would get more attention, and therefore greater support. Very calculatingly, we wrote a play that was at once "socialist-realist" and "daringly critical." We wrote it with lots of parts for our friends. Unlike *September Nights,* it didn't take place among officers; it was about ordinary soldiers, so that in fact it represented progress—we were able to get even closer to the people. Our play was called *The Life Ahead (Život před sebou)* and we had great success with it in the lower levels of competition. But when the time came to take the play to the all-army festival in Mariánské Lázně and there was a danger that we might actually win, the main political administration of the army took a close look at our personnel files and came, quite properly, to the conclusion that we were making fun of them. The Fifteenth Motorized Artillery Division stood behind us and gave us soldierly encouragement, but there was no longer anything they could do about it.

In the end, we did go to Mariánské Lázně, and we even performed the play, though not as part of the competition, merely so that we could be properly exposed for what we were. The next day, a large tribunal of sorts was held, and our play was condemned as antiarmy. An analysis of the play presented by one of the lieutenants (we later became friends; he turned into a reform communist and was constantly apologizing to me for that incident) argued, for instance, that the play did not sufficiently exalt the role of the regimental party organization, or that it was unthinkable for a Czechoslovak soldier to fall asleep while on guard duty. We found it all very funny, and we were glad to be able to spend a week in Mariánské Lázně with no regular army duties.

So that was my first encounter with theatre. I don't think it's true that I started to take a serious interest in theatre because of my wife, though it is true that, long before I was involved with the theatre, she had played in an amateur troupe, she went to the theatre regularly, and she knew more about it than I did. I became serious about theatre when I got back from the army and worked with Jan Werich. I had stopped writing poetry by this time (I'm not counting my later collections of typographical poetry) and had started writing plays. When I got back from the army, I wasn't really anything and I had no idea what I was going to do. I couldn't get into any humanities courses (my last chance had been the theatre faculty of AMU, where I had applied just before completing my term in the army), and my efforts to study at the technical university had come to nothing too. I didn't know whether to look for work in a factory, or to try to find a job that was closer to my own interests. Once again family connections helped: my father was an old friend of Jan Werich, so Werich hired me as a stagehand in the ABC Theatre.

What did that experience give you?

The season I worked in the ABC Theatre was decisive. By sheer coincidence, it was Werich's last season in the theatre. Under Werich, the ABC Theatre was a dying echo of the old Liberated Theatre, and I was fortunate enough to be able to breathe, literally at the last minute, something of its atmosphere. It was there I came to understand—because I could observe it daily from the inside—that theatre doesn't have to be just a factory for the production of plays or, if you like, a mechanical sum of its plays, directors, actors, ticket-sellers, auditoriums, and audiences; it must be something more: a living spiritual and intellectual focus, a place for social self-awareness, a vanishing point where all the lines of force of the age meet, a seismograph of the times, a space, an area of freedom, an instrument of human liberation. I realized that every performance can be a living and unrepeatable social event, transcending in far-reaching ways what seems, at first sight, to be its significance.

I recall, for example, the famous *forbíny*—dialogues between Werich and Horníček in front of the curtain during intermissions—and we all watched it every time and we always laughed, though we knew these dialogues by heart; even the musicians in Vlach's orchestra, who were pretty ignorant people, stayed in the orchestra pit to listen each evening, though they could have gone to the prop room and had a few drinks. What was it that radiated from those dialogues? What was it that enthralled everyone time and time again? It was something difficult to describe, perhaps even mysterious. Nevertheless, it was intrinsically theatrical, and it convinced me that theatre made sense. The electrifying atmosphere of an intellectual and emotional understanding between the audience and the stage, that special magnetic field that comes into existence around the theatre—these were things I had not known until then, and they fascinated me.

I had also, as I've already said, begun seriously to write plays (I say "seriously" because we'd written *The Life Ahead*, as I say, just for the fun of it), but only for myself, of course. The first was a somewhat Ionescian one-acter called *An Evening with the Family;* then I wrote the first version of *The Memorandum*. At the same time, with all the arrogance of youth, I began to write theoretical articles in *Divadlo*, a magazine devoted to theatre. I remember Werich once turning to me behind the scenes just before he went on and saying, "So, young man, you're writing about the theatre too?" I confessed that I was. "That article about Horníček and me was magnificent," Werich said. "I sent it to Voskovec in America." Then he turned and went onstage. I was inflated with pride for a week after that.

However inspiring the atmosphere in the ABC Theatre was, I was being inwardly drawn elsewhere: toward the small theatres that were springing up at the time, and particularly to the Theatre on the Balustrade. The people who worked there were closer to my own generation, and what they were doing was not just a revival of something from the past; they were looking for a new poetics. I felt I might have a better chance there to make a contribution as something more than a stagehand.

What was the situation like in theatre in the late 1950s,
about the time when the first small theatres began to appear
in Prague?

In the 1950s there were only the large official theatres—we called them the "stone theatres." Apart from the classics, or the occasional interesting performance, the only kind of thing that genuinely attracted wide audiences was satire. By that I mean more or less superficial critiques of abuses, short-comings, human weaknesses (they were called "holdovers from the past"), bureaucracy, and bribery, the kind of satire that had a certain tradition in Soviet drama. In its time, the most popular event of this kind was Jelinek's *Scandal in the Picture Gallery* in the E. F. Burian Theatre, which at the time was still called Décka, or "Theatre D." The natural assumption in such satire was that abuses could only be criticized by someone who identified with "all the positive aspects of how our society lives," and who shared the ideals that society was allegedly aspiring to. Such satires were therefore written by communists, people who sincerely identified with the government ideology and who—seeing the contradictions between their ideals and social practice—castigated the evil practices.

The small theatres and cabarets had once had a rich tradition in this country, with theatres like Dada, the Liberated Theatre, the Red Seven, and others like them, but after 1948 they vanished from our theatrical culture. The only thread connecting their world with the renaissance of the late 1950s and early 1960s was the ABC Theatre, which for a time was a genuine oasis of things that managed to escape the various ideological and aesthetic strictures of the time. They even went beyond the terms of satire, as they were then understood. The ABC was the only theatre that maintained the tradition of free humor, of poetic shorthand, clown shows and the like.

The renaissance of the small theatres occurred sometime between 1956 and 1957, when the Akord Klub began to play in Reduta. It was in fact the first—or, rather, the first well-known—rock band in Czechoslovakia, and it was an enormously interesting and important phenomenon. The leader was Viktor Sodoma, father of the famous pop singer; his wife sang, and Jiří Suchý played bass. At their late-night concerts in Reduta they played famous rock-and-roll tunes for which they had written their own lyrics, and they played their own compositions as well. Suchý, for instance, sang "The JZD Blues," "Blues For You," and many of his oldest songs. The room would only hold sixty people, but all of Prague, if I can put it that way, was jammed in. It was a sensation. I was lucky enough to discover it early on, and I was there in the crowds that jammed the room. I could sense at once that something important was going on here. I didn't understand music very well, but it didn't take much expertise to understand that what they were playing and singing here was fundamentally different from "Kristynka" or "Prague Is a Golden Ship," both official hits of the time. The novelty was not only in the music, in the rhythms of rock and roll, which was something new here then, but above all in the lyrics. Suchý's songs were evocative of many things, from the lyrics of Voskovec and Werich all the way to the poems of Christian Morgenstern. But one thing they reminded no one of: the banal lyricism of the official hits. It was an entirely different kind of fantasy, a different sense of humor, a different feeling for life, different ideas, different language. The atmosphere in Reduta was marvelous, and what was born in those sessions was that very special, conspiratorial sense of togetherness that to me is what makes theatre. That was where it all began.

The Theatre on the Balustrade was founded in 1958, when I was in the army. The director Helena Philipová was there from the beginning; in fact, she was the one who came up with the idea; she found the space, and she urged Suchý to write something that could be done onstage and would bring the atmosphere of Reduta into the theatre. Suchý got together with Ivan Vyskočil, who was very important for that whole era, and together they wrote *If a Thousand Clarinets*. To be more precise, Suchý wrote it and worked texts by Vyskočil into it. It was with this play that the Theatre on the Balustrade began. There were no professional actors in it. I saw a performance during one of my army leaves; I can't recall whether I liked it or not, but I remember being fascinated by the atmosphere of the theatre. It looked different then. In one corner of the hall there was an enormous old coal-burning stove; the first generation of those little lamps we called *kondelíky* were flickering on the walls. Many of the audience stood on the balcony outside the building and watched performances through the windows (later, when my wife was an usher, she had endless problems with this phenomenon). It was all somewhat reminiscent of a nightclub. (By the way—and I don't know exactly why this is, and someday I'm going to have to give some thought to it—an inseparable part of the kind of theatre I've been drawn to all my life is a touch of obscurity, of decay or degeneration, of frivolity, I don't know quite what to call it; I think theatre should always be somewhat suspect.) No matter how the performance turned out, one thing was certain: it was full of the joy of performance, there was freedom, pure humor, and intelligence in it; it didn't take itself too seriously, and people were delighted. In short, something new and unprecedented was born.

How did you make the move to the Theatre on the Balustrade after your season in the ABC?

I remember exactly. The magazine *Kultura 60* invited me to write something about the small Prague theatres. I wrote an article, and I'd like to quote something from it here, because I can still stand behind what I wrote twenty-six years ago.

"The young Prague theatres—the Theatre on the Balustrade, *Semafor,* and the *Rokoko*—are slowly beginning to outgrow their reputation as mere centers of intelligent fun, and are starting to be understood as a serious theatrical phenomenon. In its own way, this phenomenon is symptomatic. The point is that the need for these theatres, and their popularity, betray a deeper shift in the theatrical sensibility of our time. . . . The main feature of this theatre is its humor. It is humor of a particular type which, though it has a whole range of precursors in modern art, is new or, more precisely, unusual in today's situation. It works with abbreviation and signs, and therefore it places greater demands on the audience, so that it might even be described as intellectual humor. Its principle may be defined as absurd humor, which means that, unlike satire, which derives from the mere deformation of a real subject, this humor comes from turning the real subject on its head. . . . The central theme of these comedies is developed freely, and is of course not limited to the dimensions of real probability. For the most part it is hyperbolic or allegorical, serving some elementary idea in an either critical, social, or ethical way. And as far as theatrical technique is concerned, caricature is combined with song, dadaistic gags with sophisticated abbreviations, pyrotechnics of etymological humor with the cultivation of a kind of lapidary poeticity."

*There's a marked difference between what you wrote then
and the way* Literární Noviny, *for instance, dumped on
the* Semafor *theatre.*

I don't remember what other papers were saying about
those little theatres then, but I do know they had to be defended. It came easily to me: I was not burdened by the remains of some ideological strictures on art; and in my inner
disposition, I was entirely on the side of those theatres. But
the reason I mentioned my article is that, after it was published, the editors organized a discussion to which they invited representatives from those little theatres: Suchý,
Vyskočil, and others. That was how I came to meet these people personally. At the time, Ivan Vyskočil was head of drama
at the Theatre on the Balustrade (in the meantime, Suchý had
left the Balustrade and founded *Semafor*). Vyskočil and I arranged to meet. I lent him *An Evening with the Family,* and he
offered me a job at the Balustrade. It was a stagehand's job
again, but now I had a real chance to write and take part
creatively in the work of the theatre. Naturally I accepted it;
I wrote a nice letter to Werich explaining why I was leaving
and thanking him for everything, and in the summer of 1960
I started work at the Theatre on the Balustrade.

Thus beginning an entirely new era in your life?

Yes, that period was extremely important for me, not only
because those eight years in the Theatre on the Balustrade
were in fact the only period when I was able to devote myself
fully to theatre, to the only kind of theatre that interested me,
but also because it formed me as a playwright. I gave myself
over to my work with an almost preposterous enthusiasm; I
was in the theatre from morning to evening, and at night,
with my wife's help, we made the scenery. It was like a joyous
intoxication. After a time, I settled down and became more
down-to-earth about it, but up until 1968, when I left, I lived

for that theatre, I helped to create its profile, and I identified with it entirely. I went through a number of jobs when I was there, from stagehand to lighting technician, secretary, reader, right up to dramaturge. But it didn't really matter which of those jobs I held in any given moment, and often I held them concurrently: in the morning I organized tours, in the evening I ran the lighting for the performance, and at night I rewrote plays.

If you were asked to describe in more detail the history of the Theatre on the Balustrade and to be more precise about the role it played in Prague at the time, what sorts of things would you say, and what conclusions would you come to?

My time there can be divided in two stages. The first is tied up with Ivan Vyskočil, whose name is inseparable from the history of small theatres in the 1960s. Vyskočil was one of the godfathers of that movement. He is a distinctive personality, perhaps even eccentric, and a little self-centered, and it's hard to work with him because he finds it difficult to cooperate with anyone who's creative (he eventually argued and fell out with most of his important collaborators). The role he played still hasn't been adequately appreciated. He brought several important elements into the theatre: first, intellectual humor; second, an entirely original fantasy; third, learning (he had studied philosophy and psychology); fourth, a sense of the absurd; and fifth, a completely unconventional aesthetic impulse. He managed to link playfulness with obsession, and philosophy with humor. His need to push a playful idea to absurd extremes, and constantly to be trying something new, was infectious. He had his own theory of antitheatre or nontheatre, the denial of theatre, and he was driven by the desire to capture theatre in a state of birth. Once he explored the extent to which he could pull the audience into the performance; another time he tried to perform for himself alone. He was preoccupied with psychodrama. He was a great explorer, an upsetter, an obsessive. His influence was many-sided; for example, he came up with the idea of the Text-appeals (those very first Text-appeals following the evening performance in the Balustrade were absolutely marvelous).

As a practical man of the theatre, however, Vyskočil was impossible. He would promise plays and never bring them in (he enjoyed talking more than writing). Organizational matters didn't interest him. Sometimes his behavior was outrageous: for example, he'd say, "Tomorrow we're going to try out whatever comes into our minds," but then he wouldn't come to the rehearsal, although he was the only person in the troupe capable of that kind of creativity. He never quite seemed to realize fully the distressing fact that the theatre, among other things, is an institution that must put on a show every evening and, moreover, must do so for an audience, especially when it is financially dependent only on itself. He would hire actors randomly, without having seen them act or even talked with them, and he usually chose actors who had absolutely no understanding for this kind of theatre and who were always getting upset about things. If he had only concentrated on what amused him and left the rest to others, everything would have been all right. But he didn't want that.

It could not have turned out well. I was grateful to him for having brought me to the Balustrade, and I tried to remain loyal to him to the end, which was truly difficult, so that when we parted, unfortunately, it was not on good terms. (After I got out of prison in 1983, I went to see one of his performances and saw him for the first time in ten years. He was marvelous and behaved wonderfully toward me; perhaps time swept that ancient falling-out into the empire of forgetfulness.)

After a certain period of confusion—I think it was in the 1961–62 season—Jan Grossman was hired as head of drama, and thus began my second period with the Balustrade. I had known Grossman for some time and I respected him highly. He was a penetrating theoretician and critic, an experienced dramaturge, he had an intense relationship to the theatre,

and was aware of all the intellectual and cultural ramifica-
tions of theatre. Ultimately he became a good director as well,
and today, of course, that is all he is known for. Grossman
made of me what Vyskočil had promised, his closest artistic
collaborator. We did everything together: we chose the actors,
the plays, the directors, we sorted out the everyday working
problems of the theatre. If Ivan Vyskočil founded the Theatre
on the Balustrade and established its character, Grossman
took that initial investment and turned it into the theatre that
left its mark on the era. I was fortunate enough to have been
there, to have taken part in it and helped to create that era.

The crucial productions of that time were Jarry's *Ubu Roi,*
Beckett's *Waiting for Godot,* the classical one-act plays of Ionesco, a dramatization of Kafka's *The Trial,* and my own plays,
The Garden Party, The Memorandum, and *The Increased Difficulty
of Concentration.* That period came to an end in late 1968. Co-
incidentally, we—first myself and then Grossman—left the
theatre for nonpolitical reasons, but it's obvious that, if we
hadn't left of our own accord, we'd have been driven out
sooner or later anyway. In the new situation it would have
been impossible to continue what we were doing, and the
settling of accounts for our past would not have been long in
coming, particularly in my case, thanks to my various extra-
theatrical activities.

Apart from Fialka's Pantomime, which has been housed
in the Theatre on the Balustrade from the very beginning
until today, the dramatic component still exists today too. I've
seen some of the recent productions and I must say they were
wonderful. Nevertheless, the theatre has never regained the
meaning it had in the 1960s, with the sharp impact it had on
the consciousness and the conscience of its time.

What about other small theatres?

As far as general popularity and social resonance are concerned, *Semafor* held the first place. The work of Suchý and

Slitr created the atmosphere of that time; it was something that left its mark on our entire generation, probably forever. I recall that, at a festival of small theatres in Karlovy Vary where I had gone with the Balustrade, I saw a performance by one of the Suzannas from *Semafor* (I don't know which one it was), and I remember being overwhelmed by how completely beyond everything ideological it was, and thinking that many of the lively and perhaps important discussions (for example, between the dogmatists and the antidogmatists) taking place on the pages of *Literární Noviny* and other magazines were suddenly rendered ridiculous by this performance. Not that *Semafor* was engaging in polemic with them or parodying their discussions; it was just that what took place on the stage was completely outside all the themes these discussions raised. The performances were not about anything. They were just a series of songs, one after another, and the songs themselves were about nothing in particular, but it was the delight in performance, the rhythm, the pure fun, that seemed to make all those learned ideological debates seem fundamentally inappropriate, without much in common with real life. It was a manifestation of uncensored life, life that spits on all ideology and all that lofty world of babble; a life that intrinsically resisted all forms of violence, all interpretations, all directives. Suddenly, against the world of appearance and interpretation, here stood truth—the truth of young people who couldn't care less about any of that, who wanted only to live in their own way, to dance the way they wanted to dance, simply to be in harmony with their own nature. Our generation was the first that hadn't grown up inside the political confrontations of the 1950s; among us there were neither enthusiastic youth-union members, nor their programmatic political opponents, waiting until it all collapsed. *Semafor* seemed to be an elementary and spontaneous manifestation of the basic feelings of this first nonideological generation. The Balustrade never enjoyed the kind of general popularity that *Semafor* did. True, we had full houses every night, mostly young people, but it was a more intellectual audience, mainly students. In another sense, however, the Balustrade was more important than *Semafor:* it attempted to grasp some of the fundamental themes of the period at a deeper level and to articulate them; it was not just a shout of authenticity, but an attempt at analysis. Paravan, led by J. R. Pick, was a literary cabaret. *Rokoko,* under the leadership of Dřek Vostřel, tended to do satire and variety shows, and even though it put on several lively and professional productions, it was somehow outside this stream and was closer to what could be seen on many other stages at that time. And then of course there were the many small amateur theatres, from the Ypsilon Theatre in Liberec (which very quickly became professional, if I'm not mistaken) through the Ikska from Brno, all the way to Kladivadlo (for forerunner of today's Činoherní Studio in Ústí).

I knew these small theatres relatively well, because I had organized regular appearances for them in the Theatre on the Balustrade. In the second wave—that is, somewhat later than the first small theatres I've been talking about—two more star theatres of that same genus rose above Prague: Krejča's Theatre Beyond the Gate, and the Činoherní Klub, led by Jaroslav Vostrý. But it would take me too far beyond my original theme to talk about them. Instead, I'd like to recall something else: without in any way diminishing the social significance of the small theatres at that time, I saw this movement as an integral part of a far wider movement in society. It ran parallel with what was happening in film, for example—the New Wave of Jan Němec, Věra Chytilová, Miloš Forman, Pavel Juráček, and others. All of us were well aware of these parallels and the mutual influences that existed. There was a parallel in the visual arts as well: Medek, Koblasa, the Smidras group and other younger artists were beginning to exhibit; they were all artists who had defined themselves independently of an aesthetic or ideological confrontation with the official art of the time. In serious music there was the influential group called The New Music (Kopelent, Komorous, Kotík); in "light music," there was the arrival of Czech "big-beat," a wave which climaxed at the end of the 1960s, Milan Knížák and others organized happenings; Hiršal and Grögrová experimented in concrete poetry; Věra Linhartová, Bohumil Hrabal, Josef Škvorecký, and Vladimír Páral were all published; the plays of Josef Topol were performed in the National Theatre; the new generation of poets around *Tvář* and later *Sešity* (*Notebooks*) announced their arrival; and so on.

This invasion of "nonideological art" occurred against the background of an accelerating emancipation in the social sciences, and at the same time, it inspired this emancipation and helped to accelerate it even more. Philosophy, historiography, and other scholarly disciplines extricated themselves from their rigid, dogmatic straitjackets. And there was something else. Theatre is always a sensitive seismograph of an era, perhaps the most sensitive one there is; it's a sponge that quickly soaks up important ingredients in the atmosphere around it. These movements in the theatre have to be seen against the wider background of the general climate of those times. Life in Prague was different then. Today, on National Street on a Saturday evening, you will meet five cops, five moneychangers, and three drunks. Back then the streets were full. People knew how to entertain themselves spontaneously. They didn't just sit at home watching television, they went out. In the little bars and wine rooms you could find actors, painters, writers; wherever you went there was someone you knew. Life was somehow more relaxed, freer; it was as though there was more humor, ingenuousness, hope. People could get involved in something, go after something, take trouble with things; Prague had not yet been buried under a landslide of general apathy and turned stiff and corpselike under its weight. In other words—paradoxically—it made sense to deal with the absurdity of being, because things still mattered. And, in their own way, the small theatres reflected all that, gave expression to it, helped to create it. They were one of the important manifestations and mediators of this intellectual and spiritual process in which the society became aware of

itself, and liberated itself, and which inevitably led to the familiar political changes in 1968.

*What basic differences were there between the aesthetics of the
small theatres of the time and traditional theatre?*

I've already mentioned one of the differences: the diver-
gence, the nonideological nature of those theatres. We didn't
try to explain the world; we weren't interested in theses, and
we had no intention of instructing anybody. It was more like
a game—except that the "game" somehow mysteriously
touched the deepest nerves of human existence and social
life, and if it didn't always do this, at least it did so in its
happier moments. The humor was described as pure, as an
example of *l'art pour l'art,* as dadaistic, as being an end in
itself, but, oddly enough, this humor, which apparently had
no connections with "burning events" of the time, as that
phrase is conventionally understood, gave expression—
strangely and indirectly—to the most urgent matter of all:
what man really is. And without necessarily being intellectuals, perceptive members of the audience felt that even the
most grotesque escapade by Vyskočil touched something essential in them, the genuine drama and the genuine ineffa-
bility of life, things as fundamental as despair, empty hope,
bad luck, fate, misfortune, groundless joy.

Another important characteristic of these theatres was the
way they worked against illusion. The theatre no longer pretended that it was an "image of life." Psychologically detailed
types, characters represented in the kind of relationships they
would allegedly find themselves in real life, disappeared from
the stage. The small theatres simply wanted to show something, so they showed it; they showed it in all kinds of ways,
as it occurred to them, randomly, according to the law of
ideas. People were on the stage in their own right; they played
with each other and they played with the audience; they did

not present stories but, rather, posed questions or opened up themes. And—something I considered the most important thing of all—they manifested the experience of absurdity.

What exactly is absurd theatre? How would you define it?

Personally, I think it's the most significant theatrical phenomenon of the twentieth century, because it demonstrates modern humanity in a "state of crisis," as it were. That is, it shows man having lost his fundamental metaphysical certainty, the experience of the absolute, his relationship to eternity, the sensation of meaning—in other words, having lost the ground under his feet. This is a man for whom everything is coming apart, whose world is collapsing, who senses that he has irrevocably lost something but is unable to admit this to himself and therefore hides from it. He waits, unable to understand that he is waiting in vain: *Waiting for Godot*. He is plagued by the need to communicate the main thing, but he has nothing to communicate: Ionesco's *The Chairs*. He seeks a firm point in recollection, not knowing that there is nothing to recollect: Beckett's *Happy Days*. He lies to himself and those around him by saying he's going somewhere to find something that will give him back his identity: Pinter's *The Caretaker*. He thinks he knows those closest to him and himself, and it turns out that he doesn't know anyone: Pinter's *The Homecoming*. Obviously these are model situations of man in decline. These plays are often inspired by quite trivial everyday situations, such as a visit to friends (Ionesco's *The Bald Soprano*), pedagogical tyranny *(The Lesson)*, a woman burying herself in sand at the beach *(Happy Days)*. These are not scenes from life but theatrical images of the basic modalities of humanity in a state of collapse. There is no philosophizing in these plays as there is in Sartre, for example. On the contrary, what is expressed tends to be banal. In their meaning, however, they are always philosophical. They cannot be taken literally; they illustrate nothing. They merely point to the final horizon of our common general theme. They are not over-blown, highly impassioned, or didactic. They tend, rather, to be decadently joking in tone. They know the phenomenon of endless embarrassment. Often the characters are silent; often they run off at the mouth in stupid ways. They can be seen as outright comedies. The plays are not—and this is impor-tant—nihilistic. They are merely a warning. In a very shock-ing way, they throw us into the question of meaning by manifesting its absence. Absurd theatre does not offer us con-solation or hope. It merely reminds us of how we are living: without hope. And that is the essence of its warning. Absurd theatre, in its particular (and easily describable) way, makes the fundamental questions of the modern human dimension of Being its themes. Absurd theatre is not here to explain how things are. It does not have that kind of arrogance; it leaves the instructing to Brecht. The absurd playwright does not have the key to anything. He does not consider himself any better informed or any more aware than his audience. He sees his role in giving a form to something we all suffer from, and in reminding us, in suggestive ways, of the mystery before which we all stand equally helpless.

I've already written elsewhere about absurd theatre, and I don't want to repeat myself here. I should perhaps say, though, that absurd theatre as such—that is, as a tendency in dramatic literature—was not an explicit part of the artistic program of any of the small theatres in Prague in the 1960s, not even in the Theatre on the Balustrade, which came the closest to it of any. And yet the experience of absurdity did exist somewhere in the bowels of all those theatres. It was not merely transmitted through particular artistic influences; it was, above all, something that was "in the air." That's what I value most in absurd theatre: it was able to capture what was "in the air." And I can't resist a provocative quip here: I have the feeling that, if absurd theatre had not existed before me, I would have had to invent it.

Writing for the Stage

*If you compare the small theatres in the 1960s with what can
be seen in Czechoslovakia in the eighties, what conclusions
would you come to?*

The Theatre on a String, the Hana Theatre, the Theatre
on the Fringe, the Činoherní Klub, and several amateur
groups that have appeared in recent years—all of that is immensely important and in many ways akin to what existed in
the 1960s. Once again there is that unplanned movement from
below, that departure from the norm, the deliberate avoid-
ance of ideology, the lively and understanding audiences.
Again they are a symptom of a wider social awakening, a sign
of activity under the surface. Theatre has always been the first
to alert us to this. I follow these theatres, and I rejoice in
them. I often find myself being less critical toward them than
their own young audiences, which is obviously better than if
it were the other way around.

If I were to say how this movement today differs from the
movement I once took part in, I would have to mention a
certain predominance of "how" over "what." The cultivation
of acting skills, the cinematographic and directorial fantasy,
the so-called theatrical techniques, all seem to me far more
refined than they were in our time. From that point of view,
I suppose that our performances would seem rather clumsy
today. On the other hand, I think the theatre said more in
our time; it burrowed more deeply into the consciousness of
the time; it was more analytical, more direct, more transparent, and more emphatic in what it communicated.

There are a number of reasons for this. The main one is
probably that one can do far less today: the censors and the
bureaucrats are far more on the alert than they were in our
time, and therefore it is far more difficult to get to the heart
of the matter. This has led the small theatres to adopt an
increasingly sophisticated set of ciphers, suggestions, indirect
references, and vague parallels. Sometimes they are so refined and so convoluted that even someone as open to everything as I am can scarcely understand them.

The second reason is deeper and clearly relates to a subtle shift in the human sensibility, a shift that reaches far beyond the borders of Czechoslovakia. The 1980s are simply different from the disingenuous and transparent 1960s. Today's small theatre here is far more a theatre of situation, action, movement, metaphor, suggestion, association, feeling, than it is a theatre of ideas. The plays that these theatres mount are strange poetic collages, highly ambiguous fantasies that attempt to set the nerves tingling and evoke feelings. They appeal to the intellect far less.

The influence of these subtle shifts in the world's cultural atmosphere (or is it stratosphere?) combines, in Czechoslovakia, with the need to face up to the barbaric limitations of the country's cultural policies. The overdevelopment of external elements in theatrical expression sometimes goes hand in hand with a lack of irony towards the self, a certain seriousness, an emphaticness, even a gloominess in the way things are conveyed that are far less weighty or serious than the things we once tried to convey in a deliberately light, superficial way. I'm fond of one of Jan Grossman's sayings: theatre should be done well, he used to say, but it mustn't take itself too seriously. The main problem of Czech theatre is that is takes itself insanely seriously, yet at the same time it is not particularly well done. I don't mean that today's small theatres are not doing a good job; on the contrary, their performances are sometimes polished and honed to the precision of calligraphy. But for my taste, they sometimes take themselves too seriously. If you read some of their program notes, or the theoretical writings of their creators, the erudition in them (frequently more imitation than invention) is enough to make your head spin. And I can't help feeling there is something ridiculous about it. Anyone who takes himself too seriously always runs the risk of looking ridiculous; anyone who can consistently laugh at himself does not. I don't think we took ourselves that seriously. We didn't theorize and philosophize nearly as much about our work. Perhaps it was because we were more deeply immersed in the experience of absurdity; that may somehow have saved us. Reflecting on our general ridiculousness in the world, on our unfitness to be in the world, on our misery, our isolation, the grotesqueness of our illusions: these were agents of self-control that made it impossible for anyone to become unintentionally ridiculous. The brutality, the aggressivity, the exaggerations which some of the creators in today's small theatres use to try to break through the vicious circle of alienated human existence, to touch something authentic, can very easily push them right to the threshold of the ridiculous, simply because they are the result of a "short circuit." But no phase can just be skipped over; modern man must descend the spiral of his own absurdity to the lowest point; only then can he look beyond it. It is obviously impossible to get around it, jump over it, or simply avoid it.

I'd like to stress two things, however. In the first place, these opinions of mine may simply prove that I'm so rooted in my own aesthetics and my own experience of the world that I can't remain genuinely unprejudiced and open to what is new and different. But that is something everyone who has an opinion and is doing something risks. In the second place, these impressions of mine alter nothing in my basic sympathy for what is going on today in the small theatres. And, in any case, I haven't talked about everything that's going on, merely about some of the tendencies.

At the end of the sixties you finished a course of external study in dramaturgy at the theatre department of AMU. What did you get out of it, and what memories do you have of the department?

As I've already mentioned, I applied to get into that department when I'd finished my hitch in the army, so I wrote the entrance examinations while I was still in uniform. I remember having to analyze a play by Nazim Hikmet called *The Eccentric*, and I did this in an utterly Marxist way: I showed how the four basic laws of dialectics are realized in the play. The commission was astonished, and I'm sure Nazim Hikmet would have been astonished as well. The famous nestor of Czech dramaturgy, František Goetz, who was chairman of the admissions board, called me up at home after the test and congratulated me. In other words, I excelled in the exams, but it didn't help: I was not accepted. But there were several people in the department who brought attention to my case and went on trying to get me accepted. Later, when I was working full-time in the Theatre on the Balustrade, I naturally lost interest in going to theatre school, and when I eventually became a dramaturge myself, the desire to study dramaturgy evaporated completely. I had plenty of worries of my own.

It was at this moment that they accepted me—entirely on their own—for external study. I had to take it, on the one hand, so as not to let down those who had been pushing for years to get me accepted; and, on the other hand, out of regard for my mother, who had always wanted Ivan and myself to get a university education. I graduated with no effort whatsoever (in any case, I had no time to make a great effort) and I even graduated with a so-called red diploma—that is, with excellent marks. But, except for a few interesting lectures (by Vostrý, Stříbrný, and Hornát), I can't honestly say the school gave me much.

How many plays have you written by now? Could you give us a bibliographical overview?

Not counting *The Life Ahead,* which I've already mentioned, my first play, still juvenilia really, was a one-acter called *An Evening with the Family,* from 1959. After I went over to the Theatre on the Balustrade, I worked with Ivan Vyskočil on a play called *Hitchhiking,* which was performed in 1961. With Miloš Macourek, I wrote a cabaret play called *Mrs. Hermannova's Best Years,* which was performed, if I'm not mistaken, in 1962. I wrote several scenes for a poetic revue called *The Deranged Turtledove*, which was also performed sometime around that period.

My first independent full-length play was *The Garden Party*, which was given its premiere in the Theatre on the Balustrade in 1963. *The Memorandum* was mounted in 1965, but I had started writing it in 1960, and then rewritten it several times. In 1968 the Balustrade performed another play of mine, *The Increased Difficulty of Concentration*. I also wrote a short radio play called *Guardian Angel* in the sixties, and in 1968 the Czechoslovak Radio broadcast it, with Josef Kemr and Rudolf Hrušínský (I never actually heard it). Also I wrote a television play called *A Butterfly on the Antennae*, for which Czechoslovak Television gave me a kind of prize. They even prepared to tape it, but, thanks to the Soviet invasion, this never happened. Later it was done by West German Television. *The Garden Party* and *The Memorandum* were published sometime in the 1960s by Mladá Fronta, along with two of my essays and a collection of typographical poetry, all under the title *Protocols*. A separate edition of *The Garden Party* had already been published by Orbis, which also later brought out *The Increased Difficulty of Concentration*. All three plays came out as well as a supplement to *Divadlo* magazine, and recently they were published together in book form under the title *The Increased Difficulty*, by the Rozmluva press in London. To make this survey complete, I should also mention a film version of *The Garden Party*, which fortunately was never realized (I say "fortunately" because Barrandov Studios had hired a director whose poetics were not very close to mine); another unrealized film scenario, *Heart Beat* (with Jan Němec); a sound collage called *Bohemia the Beautiful, Bohemia Mine* created in Czechoslovak Radio but never broadcast (fortunately for the producers who had commissioned it), and *A Door to the Attic*, a revue based on texts by Ivan Sviták, and apparently performed later (I'm not sure about this) in Viola. In the 1970s— that is, when I was already banned—the first play I wrote was *The Conspirators* (1971), but I don't think it was very successful.

Next came *The Beggar's Opera* (1972), and in 1975 two one-act plays, *Audience* and *Private View*, to which I added a third, *Protest*, in 1978. All three feature the same character, Vaněk. In 1976 I wrote another full-length play, called *Mountain Hotel*. Except for *Protest*, all these plays from my "banned" period were published by 68 Publishers in Toronto under the title *Plays*. (Unfortunately, a working version of *The Conspirators* was published by mistake; it was even worse than the final version.) After my release from prison, I wrote a miniplay in 1983 called *The Mistake* (it was printed by *Svědectví*); then, in 1984, came a full-length play, *Largo Desolato*, and, in 1985, *Temptation*. Both were published in Munich by *Poezie Mimo Domov*. *Largo Desolato* was also published earlier in *Svědectví*. Considering that I've been writing plays now for twenty-six years, I haven't written a great deal. I should perhaps add that all my plays were and still are performed by various theatres in various countries of the world, and they've also been published in foreign languages.

Do you remember how you got the idea for The Memorandum *and where the word "ptydepe" comes from?*

I don't really like to admit this, but the idea for an artificial language called "ptydepe" was not mine: it came from my brother Ivan, who is a mathematician. Of course the play was my own idea, and I wrote it in my own way; I merely consulted with my brother in the passages on redundancy.

And how did you come up with the subject for The Garden Party?

In this case, the original impulse came from Ivan Vyskočil, for a change. After the shows, we'd always sit around in some wine bar, and he would talk about all the different themes, subjects, and ideas he had for plays. The fact is that he never, at least not in those days, turned any of his ideas into plays, but he did have a bottomless supply of them, and they'd always be different, because he'd be making them up as he was talking. Once he was talking about some connections or bribery or something, I don't really remember what it was, but I do know that he challenged me to tackle the subject. I did tackle it, but I don't suppose the play that eventually came out of it has anything in common with the original impulse.

Ten years ago, when you were approaching forty, you said, in a conversation with Jiří Lederer, that sooner or later there comes a time in a writer's life when he exhausts the initial experience of the world that compelled him to write in the first place, and that that moment is a vitally important crossroads: he has to decide whether he will simply go on repeating himself, or try to find his second wind. You said that you yourself had been standing on this crossroads for some time, looking for this second wind. Now that you're almost fifty, how do you feel about this?

I still think that a writer will find himself at a crossroads, probably around the age of thirty-five. At least that's how I felt it. Your first burst of writing necessarily draws on the things you've observed and felt and understood in your youth. One day, however, this initial burst drops off, runs out of steam, and you're faced with the question: What now? How should I go on? And if you don't want simply to reproduce mechanically the things you've already accomplished, you have to take a basic step. But this is very hard to do, because you feel bound by what you've already managed to understand so far, and what you've done. You are bound, in a sense, by your own literary history, and you can't simply slip out of that history and start again from the ground up. Moreover, you've become a little more modest, you've learned a few things, you've lost your literary virginity, as it were, with the wonderful arrogance, self-confidence, the still-sharp ability to see that goes with it.

I still think that this is true. But does it apply to me? Frankly, I'm not sure I have found anything like my second wind. After those first plays, which belong to that happy period of my first outburst of creativity, and which reflect my initial experience of the world, I've written quite a few other plays, some of which I'm rather fond of. But I'm still not entirely certain that I've really rediscovered myself. I can't write the way I used to write when I was young: I'm different, the times are different, and I'm interested in different things. But I don't think I would go so far as to say that aesthetically, for instance, I'm now walking on a new path. I'm still searching, in fact—searching for that second wind. Who knows whether I'll ever find it, or whether it can even be found. I mean, I don't know whether all the other things I will eventually write will not remain anchored forever in a feeling of merely searching for the lost certainty of youth—

In an incredibly short time after you finished Largo Desolato, *you finished your next play,* Temptation. *Doesn't this indicate that you've found some new approach after all? How do you feel about your two most recent plays?*

I've always taken a long time to write plays; I write slowly and with great difficulty. Usually two or three years go by between plays, and each play goes through several drafts. I would rewrite them, restructure them, worry a lot over them, and once in a while I would give in to despair. I am definitely not a spontaneous type of author. And suddenly a very strange thing happened: in July 1984 I wrote *Largo Desolato* in four days, and in October 1985 I wrote *Temptation* in ten days. Obviously something had really changed; something had happened to me. But I'm not reading too much into this, and I certainly don't intend to draw any long-range conclusions from a mere change in my working rhythm or method. It doesn't necessarily mean anything in itself, let alone promise anything for the future.

For now, I tend to think there were external factors at work. For instance, when I came back from prison, I had a bad case of nerves. I was constantly depressed and out of sorts; nothing gave me any pleasure. Everything became a duty. At the same time, I carried out these duties, both the real and the apparent ones, with a kind of surly stubborness. An Austrian critic wrote of one of my plays that it seemed to have been written out of the very depths of despair, and that it was my attempt to save myself. I laughed at his notion of how plays got written, but now I feel as though I should apologize to him: perhaps my writing these plays so soon after coming home from prison really was an act of self-preservation, an escape from despair, or a safety valve through which I sought relief from myself.

Another thing, more external but perhaps more important because of that. Among the various manifestations of obsessive neurosis that marked my condition after my return from prison (and perhaps still marks it), there is one that probably every dissident knows: fear for his manuscript. As long as the text into which you've put your best effort, or which you consider very important, is not safely hidden away somewhere, or reproduced and distributed in a sufficient number of copies, you live in constant suspense and uncertainty. And this does not improve with time: you never get used to the notion that your manuscript is constantly in danger. On the contrary, your fear becomes a genuinely pathological obsession. And if the original fear was merely of a house search, or a body search, to be allayed by giving the manuscript to the neighbors in the early-morning hours, before house searches traditionally begin, then over time your fear becomes broader and more general: you begin to fear that they will lock you up tomorrow, that you will die or become ill, simply that something undefined will happen to you (the more uncertain the fear, the more advanced the disease) that will make it impossible for the work to see the light of day. And as the work draws to completion, the suspense grows: you begin to fear that someone will trip you just before the finish line. You begin to look forward to the time when you will have nothing incomplete lying around. Prison merely makes fears of this kind more profound.

I think this played an important role in my case. I wrote both those plays with increasing impatience, in feverish haste, in a bit of a trance. This doesn't mean they're not finished: I would never allow something to leave my hands that I didn't think was finished. It merely means that an imp has taken up residence in me who forces me to finish in a hurry. When the play is done and safely tucked away somewhere, I don't care what anyone does to me. I'm happy; I feel I've triumphed over the world once more. As long as it's lying out there on my table as a practically illegible manuscript, I tremble, not just for the play but for myself—which is to say, for that part of my identity that would be irrevocably torn away from me if the manuscript were confiscated. That's really all I can say in general terms about my last two plays.

Now, about *Largo Desolato:* More than once I've used, and abused, a theme or an idea that comes from the world immediately around me, and so I've earned the silent or vocal rebuke of those who, justifiably or unjustifiably, felt hurt. I always regretted this, but I would never think of dropping such a theme, or of not doing it again. The thing is, I know I have no right to do so. When the drama demands something, I must respect its will and not censor it. If I did, I would be sinning against the very essence of my profession. The role of the writer is not merely to arrange Being according to his own lights; he must also serve as a medium to Being and remain open to its often unfathomable dictates. This is the only way the work can transcend its creator and radiate its meaning further than the author himself can see or perceive. And so—without wanting to—I have sometimes wounded or hurt someone.

In *Largo Desolato,* all those I may once have hurt can see

an instrument of divine justice taking revenge on me for them. The damage I inflict in this play is on myself, for a change. Everyone, including foreign drama critics, tries to see myself in its main character, the deranged Doctor Kopřiva, and many have felt sorry that I'm in such terrible shape. But the injunction not to censor the themes and the motifs that haunt me and inspire me is not something I can respect only when it concerns others, and then reject when I'm the one involved! I knew what I was letting myself in for, but I had no right not to let myself in for it. This play was inspired by my own experiences, certainly more directly than any other play I've written, and this is true not only of the individual motifs, but also about its most basic theme. I really did put a bit of my own instability into Kopřiva's instability, and in a certain sense it is a real caricature, containing elements of me and of my postprison despair. At the same time, it is not an autobiographical play; it is not about me, or only about me as such. The play has ambitions to be a human parable, and in that sense it's about man in general. The extent to which the play was inspired by my own experiences is not important. The only important thing is whether it tells people something about their own human possibilities. And anyway, if I was as badly off as Kopřiva, I couldn't have written a thing, certainly not with any ironic distance, so in fact the very existence of this play argues against its being autobiographical.

Regarding *Temptation:* As far as I know, I don't think anyone saw me in that play. And yet it is every bit as much inspired by my personal experience, which was even more profound and painful than the experience that lay behind *Largo Desolato* (Ivan Jirous put his finger on this in his essays on those two plays). But let me approach it somewhat systematically. The plays I wrote in the 1960s tried to grasp the social mechanisms and the situation of man crushed by these mechanisms; that is, they were—as we say today—about the "structures" and the people in them. The theme of man expelled from the structures and at the same time confronting them—in other words, the theme of dissenting opposition or resistance—did not appear. This is understandable: whether we like it or not, we always take off—regardless of how far we wish to fly—from the ground we know. I was "within the structures" then (that my "view from outside" particularized the structures in one way or another is another matter). At the time I had no dissident experience—at least not in the form it took in the 1970s. Later, when I was expelled from the structures and found myself a dissident, I naturally began to explore that situation and examine it in different ways (including the very same "view from outside")! In other words, the ground from which I took off had changed. From this arose the series of Vaněk plays, three one-act plays that finally led to *Largo Desolato,* which examines what happens when the personification of resistance finds himself at the end of his tether.

After *Largo Desolato,* I didn't think I could go any further in that direction. I suddenly felt the need to begin in a completely different way, to draw from another barrel, to abandon the terrain of dissident experience (which in any case was suspected, somewhat unjustifiably, of being too exclusive). In short, I didn't want to depend so transparently on my own experience; I was tired of hearing yet again that dissidents could only write about themselves. Therefore, I decided to try writing about the structures again, as though I were inside them. I intentionally tried to re-create, to some extent, the atmosphere of my old plays. I was curious to see what would come out of it now, face to face with the present, after everything that had happened in the meantime. That was how I found the territory. What was to fill it up, however, has its own, deeper roots.

Ever since 1977, when I was first imprisoned, I'd been haunted by the Faust theme; it was in the air around me. I wasn't in jail for long that time, but even so, for various reasons, it was a difficult time for me. I didn't know what was going on outside; I could only follow the hysterical campaign against Charter 77 in the newspapers. I was deceived by my interrogators and even by my own defense lawyer. I was buffeted by strange and somewhat psychotic states and feelings. I had the feeling that, as one of the initiators of the Charter, I had hurt many people and brought terrible misfortune upon them. I took upon myself an inordinant share of the responsibility, as though the other Chartists hadn't known what they were doing, as though I alone were to blame.

In this miserable state of mind, I began to understand, toward the end of my stay in prison, that a trap was being laid for me: a relatively innocent turn of phrase—or so I thought at the time—in one of my requests for release was to be published in a falsified version in order to discredit me. I had no idea how to stop this from happening, or how to defend myself against it. It was a very dark time for me, but then odd things began to happen. If I remember correctly, instead of the usual books, like *Far from Moscow,* I suddenly had delivered to my cell Goethe's *Faust,* and then, right after that, *Doctor Faustus* by Thomas Mann. I had strange dreams and was haunted by strange ideas. I felt as though I were being, in a very physical way, tempted by the devil. I felt that I was in his clutches. I understood that I had somehow become involved with him. The experience of having something misappropriated in this way—something I had actually thought and written, something that was true—clarified for me with fresh urgency that the truth is not simply what you think it is; it is also the circumstances in which it is said, and to whom, why, and how it is said. This is one of the themes of *Temptation.* (I've analyzed this experience at some length in my letters from prison, in letters 138 and 139.)

That was when the idea to work this Faustian material up in my own way first came to me. I returned to it several times, but I always threw out what I'd written. In fact, right up to the last minute, I simply did not know how to approach that multifaceted and essentially archetypal theme. Then, last October, I got an idea and began to play with it, to sketch it in my usual fashion, first with graphs of the entrances and exits, the scenes and the acts; then I wrote it. I actually did write the whole play in ten days. So that was how *Temptation* was written. Perhaps I have found, through this play, a new starting point; perhaps I've rediscovered myself; perhaps it is really the beginning of a new stage in my writing. A number of people have told me it's my best play, but I truly can't be the judge of that. Or perhaps, on the contrary, it's just a recapitulation of something I've already dealt with, a kind of personal revival, a résumé of what has already been. I don't know. All I can do is stand behind what I've already told you about this eternal search for a "second breath."

You say that the Faust theme had been haunting you for a long time and that you didn't dare tackle it, or didn't quite know how to deal with it. Are there any other themes that haunt you and that you haven't yet dared to tackle? After this Faust, I find no difficulty in imagining that you might give us a reworked or boiled-down Don Quixote—

Nothing since has impinged upon me quite as strongly. Occasionally I've played with the idea of using other characters, like Don Juan, Oblomov, and their like, and I've even considered throwing a number of characters like that into a single play and having them confront each other. But I've given up such ideas for the time being. Right now I'm working on something else—

Who do you write for, now that you don't have your own theatre, director, or dramaturge, and when you don't even know who your audience is? How have you come to terms with that situation?

It's very trying, worse than when a poet or a novelist can't publish in his own country. A play is bound, to a far greater extent, to the "here" and a "now." It is always born out of a particular social and spiritual climate, and it is directed at that climate. That is its home, it needs that home, and it only truly becomes itself when it can be seen in that home as theatre. As a text it's incomplete. For the past seventeen years I've been deprived of these basic conditions, and, understandably, it doesn't make writing any easier. I come to terms with it by simply not admitting that this is the situation, by writing as though my plays could still be performed in the Theatre on the Balustrade and as though my contemporaries could still see them here today. By the way, I've just recently realized that to this day my plays remain faithful to the dimensions of the stage on which they were once played and the dimensions of the company that once played them. So, in fact, I'm still writing for local actors and a local public.

Do you follow the official domestic dramatic literature? For example, do you know the plays of Karel Steigerwald?

I know Karel Steigerwald, I know his plays, and I know other authors who in my opinion are very interesting, authors who have not fallen, or have not been driven into our "dissident ghetto" (perhaps because they are too young to have got mixed up in what we did earlier), and are therefore formally allowed to publish and be produced, even though they have constant problems and tend to be occasionally tolerated rather than consistently supported. If I hesitate to name names and talk about specific works, my reason is an entirely external one: I don't want to harm them.

You are in the situation of someone who has been persecuted for some time, a situation that not infrequently leads to a kind of self-worship. How do you fight against this danger? Doesn't it present a threat to your creative work as well?

I don't feel threatened by that particular danger. It has to do with my nature, my disposition, my general type, both as an author and as a man. I'm the kind of person who is always doubting himself. I'm far more sensitive to critical voices than I am to voices that praise me. I hear many different expressions of sympathy, solidarity, respect, and admiration; some have even invested their hope in me. People I don't know call me up and thank me for everything I'm doing. I'm delighted by such voices, of course, because they confirm that our efforts have some resonance, that we are not just crying out in the wilderness. At the same time, however, I always find them somewhat embarrassing, and I continually ask myself whether I really deserve such attention, whether I'll manage not to disappoint all those expectations and live up to all those demands. After all, what have I really accomplished? I've written a few plays, a few articles, I've done some time in prison. I ask myself these questions, and I harbor these feelings, so perhaps the danger of self-worship you raise is not my problem. But I could be wrong; something like that is probably best judged by the people around me.

If you're so full of fears, doubts, and questions, are you sometimes afraid of old age and death as well?

You may be surprised to hear this, but I'm not. I dream about old age as a time of rest, when nothing more will be expected of me. What bothers me more than anything else about death is that I won't be able to see how things here will turn out.

What does a person need to become a writer? How would you reply to my fifteen-year-old son, Ondřej, if he asked you that question?

The older I get, and the more experience I have, the less capable I feel of answering questions like that. There were times when, in the supreme confidence of youth, I would have been prepared to give a broad and lengthy answer. Those times, alas, are gone; I'm more modest now, and I recognize how misleading any kind of general statements about writing can be, and how easily they can be disproved. What does one need to become a writer? First of all, he should know his own language and respect it, although not even that is unequivocal. Vlasta Třešňák used to have a mistake in every sentence, yet he's a better writer than many who know Czech as well as Pavel Eisner did. When young authors show me their texts, I usually stress the importance of diligence and hard work. But of course that is merely situational advice, coming from the discovery that young authors often imagine writing to be simpler than it is: they tend to be consumed by feelings that seem immensely important and unusual, and they think that all they have to do is write it all down. I remember something Zdeněk Urbánek once said. I asked him why he thought the poems that Ivan Jirous wrote in Valdice Prison appealed to everyone, from long-haired "undergrounders" to respectable elderly gentlemen. He said it was probably because, although Jirous is expressing the existential experience of the Czech cultural underground, he does it thoroughly, not with the kind of slack approximation and offhandedness with which others do it. I can't help it: a certain tough-mindedness is obviously necessary, and that costs something. Writing is not just another job, another activity. I don't think I could say anything to your son right off the cuff. I'd have to read something he's written, and then perhaps I'd be able to draw his attention to some aspects he should be paying attention to.

In the West it's often said that the anxiety of the modern artist comes from the feeling that modern society doesn't need him. Have you ever, as a Czech writer, had this feeling of not being needed? Or have you ever thought about how the Czech version of "not being needed" differs from the Western version?

I would say that in Czechoslovakia the problem is just the opposite: here so many demands are placed on the writer that they become a burden. Traditionally in our circumstances, more is expected of writers than merely writing readable books. The idea that a writer is the conscience of his nation has its own logic and its own tradition here. For years, writers have stood in for politicians: they were renewers of the national community, maintainers of the national language, awakeners of the national conscience, interpreters of the national will. This tradition has continued under totalitarian conditions, where it gains its own special coloring: the written word seems to have acquired a kind of heightened radioactivity—otherwise they wouldn't lock us up for it! Many of our Western colleagues might envy us the degree of attention and social resonance that we enjoy. But it's a double-edged thing: it can bind one, tie one down, limit one. It's as though he were suddenly blocked by his social role, as though, out of respect for the role assigned to him and doubts about his worthiness for it, his voice acquired a stammer; as though he were simply no longer as free as he should be.

I admit that I occasionally have the desire to cry out: I'm tired of playing the builder's role, I just want to do what every writer should do, to tell the truth! Or: You can't go on expecting hope to come from professional suppliers, you have to find it first of all in yourselves! Or: Take your own risks; after all, I'm not your savior! But I always bite my tongue before I speak, and remind myself of what Patočka once told me: the real test of a man is not how well he plays the role he has invented for himself, but how well he plays the role that destiny assigned to him. It's debatable, of course, what we invent for ourselves and what we don't. In one sense, we've invented everything for ourselves: we've taken one small step forward ourselves, but this small step logically demanded further actions, which, although in a sense they go on without us, would probably never have happened without that first step. Do we really have a right to complain?

III

Facing the Establishment

*I'd like to go back just a little bit. In 1965 you became a
member of the editorial board of* Tvář, *a cultural monthly for
young writers which was later banned in rather dramatic
circumstances. What was it really like then, and what were
you personally able to do within the Writers' Union?*

I've already mentioned the strange antipathy I felt toward
the Writers' Union in the 1950s; it didn't go away in the more
liberal 1960s. That was why I never tried to become a member,
not even when my plays were already being performed and I
could have been admitted into the Union. A stronger reason
was that I was fully occupied with the theatre. In short, I didn't
see any need to take part in the writers' organization.

If I'm not mistaken, it was at the Third Writers' Union
Congress, in 1963, that Jiří Gruša asked for permission to establish a magazine for young writers, and the Union in fact
agreed. The magazine was *Tvář. Květen* had been founded in
the same way after the Second Congress. *Tvář* was run by
Gruša, Pištora, Vinant, and other young literati. I didn't know
any of them and, to tell you the truth, I felt a certain inner
distance from that whole group or generation. While I was
being a lab assistant or building pontoon bridges or working
as a stagehand, unable to get into any school and therefore a
part of the underground culture of those times, these fellows,
who were only slightly younger than I was, had come of age
in a different time. They had graduated from decent high
schools and gone on to universities, where they studied literature, and then went straight into jobs with publishing
houses and magazines. They had all published early and

quickly become members of the Writers' Union and sat around in the club. In short, they had it a little easier than I did. No doubt I envied them their decent education; but I felt they'd become official a little too soon, probably because of the alacrity with which they'd made themselves at home in this unsympathetic Writers' Union. I'm doing them an injustice, I know, but that was how I felt at the time.

I only visited the editorial offices of *Tvář* once, more out of curiosity than anything else, with several typographical poems. They made me feel welcome, they printed my poems, and they even published an article I wrote later, but I had no further contact with them. After they were in existence for about a year, a revolution of sorts took place in the *Tvář* editorial board. I was not familiar with the details and I wasn't interested: such controversies have always been a part of literary life and literary groupings.

My real association with *Tvář* began when the new editorial board, apparently at the suggestion of Jan Lopatka, invited me to join them. This invitation was not entirely free of ulterior motive. *Tvář* was a Union periodical, yet no one on the new editorial board was a Union member. Not only was the magazine constantly being chastised for this by the Union organs, but this state of affairs was also impractical, since there was no one on the magazine to keep track of what was going on in the different Union committees and defend the magazine when problems arose. The chances were good that the Union would accept me as a member, and so my invitation to join the editorial board of *Tvář* was somewhat conditional on my joining the Writers' Union and struggling there in *Tvář*'s behalf. In other words, the invitation to join *Tvář* was *de facto* an invitation to join the Union.

I knew all this—no one had tried to hide the utilitarian aspects of the invitation—and I accepted because, as I quickly found out after a few preliminary meetings with the new editorial board, their aims appealed to me in every way, and in fact were close to mine. This was something quite new in the Writers' Union; it was the only grouping of people on Union territory that I felt I could work with and identify with, with-out any inner reservations. It was a step that turned out to be far more important in my life than it first appeared to be. It was the beginning of the period, which lasted for several years, during which *Tvář* struggled for its existence; it was also the beginning of my "rebellious" involvement with the Writers' Union, also lasting several years; at the same time, it was the beginning of something deeper—my involvement in cultural and civic politics—and it ultimately led to my becoming a "dissident." I began as a kind of working stiff at the Theatre on the Balustrade, someone who lived only for his work in the theatre, and was no more than a curious observer of any-thing beyond that. Thanks to *Tvář*, I stepped outside this cir-cle, without really knowing where the inner logic of the step would take me.

I don't mean to suggest that I regretted it. On the contrary, had it not been for *Tvář*, I would have had to do the same thing in a different way sooner or later anyway, because I can't imagine myself remaining enclosed within the horizon of a single small theatre forever. That would have gone against my nature, and it wouldn't have helped my writing either, though some have tried to persuade me that, if I'd stuck to writing plays and not got mixed up in other things, I would have done better and could have written incomparably more plays. I don't believe that's right, and the fate of more than one of my colleagues confirms that this attempt to devote oneself to literature alone is a most deceptive thing, and that often, paradoxically, it is literature that suffers for it. When I joined the editorial board of *Tvář*, my involvement in the struggle for the magazine's survival began. It was a period of endless debates, meetings, and arguments; it was my private school of politics.

Let me try to sketch in the situation as it was then. In the Central Committee of the Writers' Union, in the publishing houses and editorial offices and boards, in the whole institu-tional base of literature, communists naturally had the last word, but by this time—the mid-sixties—they were reform communists or revisionist communists. We called them the "antidogmatics." By this we simply meant those whose efforts, which often involved difficult and protracted conflicts with the Novotný bureaucracy, finally issued in the Prague Spring. These people formed something like the cultural establishment of the time. Many of their efforts, of course, were allied to ours—the younger noncommunist writers. They were a better alternative than the aging Novotný bureaucracy and its notorious dogmatists. Still, from our point of view, these people had their limitations (today, it must be said, most of them no longer do). We found many elements in their behavior problematic: they still harbored many illusions; they were still beholden to the old ideological schemata; they constantly thought in terms of tactics; they were inconsistent and sometimes almost childish; and they automatically identified with their own "establishment" positions, which they took as a matter of course. It was inconceivable to them that anyone else might have something to say about what they were doing. They had the tendency to extend their own experience of the world to include everyone else. For example, they would always speak of themselves as a generation, and not as merely a particular part of that generation—in this case, young party members. When this entire stratum of intellectuals was swept away after the Soviet invasion, they were accused, by various bitter hacks who grasped the historical opportunity and occupied the empty places in the literary establishment, of "elitism." I don't think I'll be harming anyone, and certainly not insulting anyone today, if I say that there really was a touch of elitism in the behavior of this "antidogmatic establishment," though I mean it in quite a different sense from that of the hacks who took their places.

Tvář was the first case in which something that was grounded in an institution was not in the hands of this establishment. It was a tiny, almost insignificant oasis, to be sure, but it was an oasis of something different. Not because *Tvář* was deliberately anti-Marxist or anticommunist: politically, and intellectually as well, *Tvář* was in no way clearly defined, at least not in the sense that it declared its support for some ideological doctrine. It was just that the ideological debates of the time somehow passed over it, perhaps in somewhat the way they passed over the small theatres I've talked about, or the New Wave in film, and many other phenomena of that period that are connected with the arrival of a younger generation. *Tvář* simply printed what its editors considered good, interesting, profound, authentic—from Heidegger to Teilhard to Trakl, Jan Hanč, and Jiří Kuběna—and they didn't really worry about where people placed the magazine. But their choice of authors and their taste revealed a different experience and a different background, unconnected, even by the slightest of umbilical cords, to any earlier ideological points of view. Our points of departure were different, and we even had a different aesthetic: we didn't like much of what the antidogmatics liked and, on the contrary, we liked a lot that they didn't like. I wouldn't say that *Tvář* was a small island of "non-Marxism" in a sea of (reform) Marxism, but I would say that, from our point of view, it was an island of freedom in an ocean of something that thought of itself as immensely free but in fact was not.

For the "antidogmatic establishment" that ran the Writers' Union, the fact that one Union magazine was beyond their control like that was of course very hard to take. They felt they shouldn't be publishing something that was so far from their way of thinking and, what was more, something they could not possibly defend before the bureaucracy. This reluctance was merely reinforced by the fact that, in almost every issue of *Tvář,* one of the best-sellers of the period, was mercilessly torn to shreds. The leading people in the Union must have felt that they were paying for their own liquidation. From the outset, therefore, the mood in the Union was against *Tvář,* which made it necessary, from the very first day, to fight in *Tvář*'s behalf.

*Well, you could read all that from the polemics in the press.
Jiří Sotola, for example, in* Literární Noviny *for September 4,
1965, attacked your article in* Plameny #7 *on art. His reply
is swarming with expressions like "barking," "a slap in the
face," "primitive manners," "vulgarity," "excommunication
from literature," "rubbing things out," and so on. A few
weeks later, On October 16, 1965, Jan Trefulka wrote an article on* Tvář *in* Literární Noviny, *and he put it very precisely: "No threat of a ban should hang over the heads of
people and magazines that do not consider themselves Marxist in the strict and limited sense of the word, if they clearly
and precisely state their positions. . . ."*

You see, that's a perfect example of why antidogmatic
thinking seemed incredibly naïve to us. Trefulka was trying
to tell the party bureaucracy (everything the antidogmatics wrote they wrote to "educate" their superiors) that they
should leave us alone, but because he knew it wasn't going to
be that simple, he offered a compromise: we were to come
out and say exactly what we were. But such a thing can only
be suggested by someone who subscribes to an ideology and
believes that anyone who doesn't subscribe to it must therefore subscribe to another ideology, because he can't imagine
anyone's not subscribing to an ideology. What could we have
said, to "clearly and precisely" state what we were? I have no
idea. But even if we could and were willing (of course we were
against it) to declare our admiration for some other ism—for
example, existentialism—it would have meant digging our
own grave! If the bureaucracy can't classify something, it can
tolerate it for some time. Once it has it classified (remember
the cultlike importance of terminology under communism!),
it wastes no more time with it. At the risk of angering my
friend Trefulka, I must say this: everyone who does not identify with the ruling ideology knows very well how carefully he
would have to behave if he were to "clearly and precisely"
declare himself, yet not be swept away. The kind of suggestion
Trefulka made could only have been made by someone who

sees the world "from above"—this is, from the balcony of official ideology—and who knows nothing of the elementary experiences of those "below."

But back to *Tvář*. I remember the beginning of my struggle very well. In 1965 there was a conference of the Writers' Union on the occasion of the twentieth anniversary of the liberation. Black clouds were already gathering above *Tvář*, and my friends and I decided that the best defense was attack. I wrote an incendiary speech in which I said many harsh things about the Writers' Union, and particularly that this anniversary could best be marked by the Union's taking a critical look at itself. I pointed out the rampant bureaucratism, and inflexibility, the intolerance, the number of wonderful authors who were senselessly excluded from literature and whom the Union was incapable of pardoning. And I explained to them why *Tvář* had a right to life.

My speech was given an enormous round of applause— God knows why, since it was directed against a majority of the applauders. It was my first appearance before a writers' organization since the meeting in Dobříš in 1956, and the effect was just as scandalous. I more or less broke the conference up, but in a way that no one could very well argue against. Pavel Auersperg, who was there for the party, apparently told Jan Procházka after my speech: "He's going to be a dangerous fellow for us." Although I've never had the ambition to be a professional conference-destroyer, I must say that I was flattered. The main thing, of course, was that our maneuver worked. They left *Tvář* alone for a while. In the end, though, banning became more and more inevitable. The Central Committee of the Union had to make it appear as though they were doing it on their own initiative, but in fact they were ordered to do it by the Central Committee of the Communist Party. Left to themselves, the antidogmatics would not have banned us, but we weren't worth a rebellion inside the party, so they did it anyway. Of course, they explained it to us in their traditional antidogmatic way: The struggle for great things—the general liberalization of conditions—demands minor compromises in things that are less important. It would not be tactical to risk an open conflict over *Tvář*, because there is bigger game at stake. (In 1968 Smrkovský argued in exactly the same way to justify having voting for the liquidation of *Literární Noviny* in 1967; and later Husák, in exactly the same way, would argue for the exclusion of Smrkovský from the political scene. This is a model of self-destructive politics.)

We argued that the best way to liberalize conditions is to be uncompromising precisely in those "minor" and "unimportant" details, such as the publication of this or that book or this or that little magazine. Our argument was not heard. Nevertheless, a kind of hangover from this experience remained in antidogmatic circles. And it began to spread rapidly when we refused to accept their ultimatum silently, and refused to accept the rules of the game as they had played it until then. We began to defend ourselves. First we organized a petition of writers protesting against the decision of the Union's Central Committee. If I recall correctly, about two hundred writers signed it. That was the first blow to the antidogmatic establishment. Those who had seen themselves as standard-bearers of progress were now being accused of reactionary behavior by their own membership! That petition was followed by another, demanding an extraordinary congress of the Union. According to the statutes, if a third of the membership sign the petition, a congress must be held. The authors of the statutes, of course, had never dreamed that what they'd written might ever be taken literally, which is probably why they left the clause in, and why there are so many other democratic clauses in the laws and statutes, including the Constitution: to keep up appearances, and in the belief that no one would ever dare behave as though they were real.

We began to gather signatures, and it was soon clear that there was a real danger we'd actually get that third. Then what would they do? Hold a congress just because a couple of hooligans decided they wanted one? Or spit publicly on the statutes? It was a precarious situation for the party to be in, and it put forth an enormous effort to dissuade writers from signing the petition. Groups of writers were invited to have coffee at Central Committee headquarters, where they were promised the sky and told that they could publish practically whatever they wanted. Auersperg, who was head of the cultural department, dealt with me. It was like a summit of two opposing parties. If I withdrew the petition, he said, I would be given my own magazine (minus the main people on the editorial board of *Tvář*, of course, but they would be allowed to publish in it), but I couldn't have stopped it even if I'd wanted to. As it turned out, I didn't get the required number of signatures, which given the state of things was only to be expected.

Still, I think our efforts had a great importance, one that has not been recognized, even today. We introduced a new model of behavior: don't get involved in diffuse general ideological polemics with the center, to whom numerous concrete causes are always being sacrificed; fight "only" for those concrete causes, and be prepared to fight for them unswervingly, to the end. In other words, don't get mixed up in backroom wheeling and dealing, but play an open game. I think in this sense we taught our antidogmatic colleagues a rather important lesson; their hangover became more profound and ultimately led to a strange recantation of their original decision, which came too late to change anything. But they had come to understand something important. They realized that many of their former methods were hopelessly out of date, that a new and fresher wind was blowing, that there were people—and there would obviously be more and more of them—who would not be stopped in their tracks by the argument that a concrete evil was necessary in the name of an abstract good. In short, I think that *Tvář* had an educational effect on the antidogmatic members of the writing community. Suddenly here was the party taking us, a handful of fellows, more seriously than the entire antidogmatic "front." And they were taking us more seriously for the simple reason that we could not be so easily talked out of our convictions. I'm saying all this is in the interest of historical truth, not because I want to draw attention to any personal merit. In any case, my role in all this was that of an executor; the strategy was the collective creation of *Tvář*, and I am extremely grateful to the magazine for that whole experience.

But to return to the facts: the regular Writer's Union Congress was drawing near, and the party felt that the main danger lay in *Tvář*. It was afraid that we would "wreck the congress." The magazine had been banned, but now the wooing began. I was named to a committee charged with preparing the congress. I refused on the grounds that I could not prepare a congress for an institution that had banned our magazine. They replied that the magazine would be permitted again if the congress turned out well. I had my own opinion about such assurances. The secretary of the Union invited me to his own home, tried to get me drunk and then pry information from me about "what we were up to." I had to laugh to myself. After all, our approach—which was to demand concrete things, books, magazines, democratization within the Union, etc., etc., and not to get mixed up in political discussions, which always involve some compromise with the powers that be, or at least the acceptance, for the sake of discussion, of some of their sacrosanct dogmas and a certain form of language—was a constructive approach that in no way threatened to evoke a national or international scandal!

And, indeed, everything turned out differently. The Fourth Writers' Union Congress did in fact lead to a split in the party, but it was not our doing. The congress was "broken up"—in other words, became a forum in which the truth could be spoken—by the antidogmatics themselves, our colleagues from the *Literární Noviny* circle. In other words, the blow came from an unexpected quarter. Once again the party had assessed the situation badly. It had noticed that *Tvář* had set something in motion, and therefore it expected the blow to come from that direction. But what *Tvář* had set in motion—in the best sense of the word—were those whom the party had considered more pacifiable: the progressive communists. Many may disagree with me, but I claim that, if *Tvář* had not done what it did, the progressive communists would not have become radicalized to the extent that they did. I claim that, in some regard, they pulled themselves together thanks to the lesson that *Tvář* taught them. Of course, Ludvík Vaculík spoke to the congress the way he did because he had decided to manifest the truth of his thinking, not because he was trying to "outdo" *Tvář* in courage. These things don't happen quite so simply. What does happen, though, is certain hidden shifts in the communal spiritual and moral sensibility, and subtle atmospheric changes whose causes they may not be aware of, but which have their impact all the same. At least that was how I saw it and experienced it.

The antidogmatics launched their attack in their own way. They did not adapt to the strategy put forward by *Tvář*. Their appearance at the congress ended in precisely the kind of global political confrontation that we had tried to avoid, although it was considerably more open and more principled than all such confrontations before, which had always been hopelessly mired in compromise. At the time, we didn't quite know what to think of it. We were delighted that someone had spoken the truth (or at least had taken a large step closer to it), and we were delighted that, after such brave and frank statements, there could be no return to those backroom decisions and deals about what to sacrifice in order that something else be saved. But our delight was tempered by doubts about whether direct confrontation on the political level would lead anywhere, and by fears that it could simplify a counterattack by the power center. To this day, I don't have a clear opinion about this.

It's certain that the Fourth Congress, simply by unfolding the way it did, accelerated developments, and was the immediate curtain-raiser to the Prague Spring. This would suggest that what was done was correct. On the other hand, although truth was spoken at the congress, it was not spoken in its entirety, and the question is: did this not prefigure certain essential inner contradictions in the antidogmatists' position that in the end made them easier to suppress? Perhaps the small percentage of the truth that remained unexpressed was the embryo of that fatal schizophrenia of 1968. That would seem to suggest that our fears at the time were more justified than our delight. But I can't decide myself, and I leave the final judgment to those better qualified.

If I have been putting the emphasis on the unappreciated "cultural-political" significance of *Tvář*, this does not mean that *Tvář* was not an interesting magazine in its own right. Even today, it reads better than most literary magazines from that period, including *Literární Noviny*. Nor does it now provoke any of the indignation among some of our communist colleagues that it once did. It's paradoxical, but obviously this hard time had to come in order for many intellectuals to shake off the last of their ideological prejudices. Even though we are all different (and I hope this will remain), we have become extraordinarily close in one thing: in the importance we attach to lack of prejudice and inner freedom. In that regard, the tiny oasis of *Tvář* was a precursor; *Tvář* was pointing in the right direction.

But it's time to stop praising *Tvář* and mention some of the things that were bad about it. From the outset, there was an element of sectarianism in it, and this grew to more serious proportions as time went on. Fortunately, it was not visible on the pages of the magazine itself, but it was more than obvious behind the scenes. I don't know to what extent this was a necessary price to be paid for playing the kind of role *Tvář* played, and to what extent it was simply excessive; in other words, I don't know to what extent the sectarianism was a result of the conditions in which *Tvář* had to operate and defend itself, or whether it was a purely internal problem. But the fact is that *Tvář* too had its "inner sanctum," the tightest circle being around its spiritual leader, Emanuel Mandler. This group made all the decisions in advance and shamelessly manipulated the editorial board as a whole. In other words, *Tvář* too had its trials, its heretics, its discipline, its dogmas, etc. I myself had two falling-outs with *Tvář;* after the first break, I made my peace with the magazine again and even became chairman of the editorial board; the second time, in 1969, I broke with them for good. And some of my friends, before me or after me, broke with them too, and it was no accident that they were all writers of belles lettres—that is, people who, perhaps more stubbornly than others, guard their own independence (Zdeněk Urbánek, Věra Linhartová, Josef Topol, Ladislav Dvořák, and there may have been others as well; I can't recall all the ins and outs of that period). The era of internal controversy began rather curiously. One day we came to a meeting of the editorial board. At that time, *Tvář* was not being published, but *Sešity* had been established on its grave and was therefore roundly and justifiably condemned by *Tvář*. We arrived at the meeting to discover that the inner sanctum planned to hold a kangaroo court with Milan Nápravník because he'd promised to let *Sešity* publish one of his texts. Those of us on the editorial board who had not been told of it beforehand, including myself, realized how foolish this approach was, but our improvised attempts to stop the "trial" were brilliantly foiled by the machinery of this well-prepared inner sanctum. Nápravník took this all with quiet disdain (perhaps, as a former surrealist, he was used to such things), and in the middle of the proceedings he went to weigh himself on a set of bathroom scales that happened to be in the room where we were meeting. This—making light of the whole meeting—was considered an even more serious offense than his intention to publish one of his texts in *Sešity*.

I slammed the door on *Tvář* the moment I discovered they were putting me in the dock too. Apparently, when speaking at the constitutional congress of the Czech Writer's Union (this was after the Union had been federalized, I had deviated from the line that *Tvář* had established and made binding on all members of its group. It is sad that *Tvář* fell more and more deeply into the same mannerisms it had struggled so courageously against for so long. It recalls Eugene O'Neill's famous statement: "We fought so long against small things that we became small ourselves."

Another question about your involvement with the Writers' Union: didn't you hold positions in the Union later on that had nothing to do with Tvář?

There was one thing I couldn't stand about the Writer's Union then: almost everyone complained about having to hold office, almost everyone said it was important to write, not have meetings. They'd make a great show of being bored, and during meetings they'd usually sit at the bar in the adjoining room, turning their noses up at everything. At the same time, they stuck it out; it never occurred to anyone simply to resign from office, go home, and write. They were all trembling, anxious to be elected to office once more. This was understandable: holding on to an office in the Writers' Union had a direct influence on whose books got published, on the size of the print run, on the awarding of literary prizes, on who got named to various delegations, on grants, and so on. In other words, there were perks to be had. What really annoyed me was this ambiguity: they were anxious to hold these positions, yet turned their noses up at them. It wouldn't have bothered me so much if that attitude had not really mattered. But it did matter: occasionally some pretty important matters were discussed—for example, who could be a member of the Union and who could not (for many people this was an important existential question)—yet, instead of taking part in such meetings, instead of trying to help someone, instead of trying to do something good, these people would sit around at the bar drinking. That seemed immoral to me. But it was typical for people in that milieu.

I felt that, if they found these functions boring, they ought to resign; or, if they really wanted to hold these offices, they should carry out their responsibilities in a proper manner for the general good. Simply to use them as a source of personal

advantage and not as an obligation to do something useful—
that I could not approve of. Now, in the several years I worked
in the Writers' Union, my rebellion—what else could it have
been—was founded on a fierce, stubborn, and often inept
attempt to do things differently. So that, whenever I was asked
to do something, or named to a committee or something, I
put my whole heart into it. I stuck my nose into everything, I
came to meetings prepared, I discussed every aspect of every
question, I was always criticizing abuses and making proposals. My agility, oddly enough, did not result in their driving
me out as a disruptive element; on the contrary, they gave me
even more work to do. They got used to my big nose, they
were glad to have somebody there who did more than just
sleep and raise his hand when he had to. Without really wanting to, I became something like a standard they could measure themselves against, and they probably decided it would
be better to have someone like me involved in the Union
rather than working behind their backs, because then they'd
never know where he might attack them from.

As I've already said, one of the first things I did in the
Union was fight to save *Tvář*, and in the process I may have
actually gained some respect, albeit a controversial respect.
This led imperceptibly to other responsibilities, ones that had
nothing directly to do with *Tvář*. But once you say A, you
must also say B. When I said, for instance, that the Writers'
Union was a clumsy bureaucratic organization, completely
and nonsensically modeled after the Communist Party, they
would say, all right, suggest some reforms. If I'd refused, I
would have become a bit of a flake. So I had to come up with
a proposal for a new set of statutes. And so it went. To some,
I may well have seemed like a comic figure, the eternal busy-
body, cultivated and tolerated to keep things from getting too
boring, but I didn't mind. As a matter of fact, I even enjoyed
playing that role. But the main reason was that I felt I could
do some good in the Writers' Union. I have no idea anymore
how many actual victories I scored; some, perhaps. For example, I'm sure that some writers were accepted as members

of the Union who perhaps otherwise would not have been accepted.

In 1968 the noncommunists—that is, people who were not members of the party—began to rouse themselves. In that atmosphere, they were able to make themselves heard and to demand that they be accepted on equal terms with communists. They were, after all, the majority, yet they remained second-class citizens, because all the important positions were held by communists, and all the most important decisions were made by the party behind closed doors. The program of reform communism could provide no clear answer to the problem of what to do with non–party members. They could only come up with dialectical evasions. But noncommunists were demanding to take part in public life. They felt a need for their own institutionalized structures. The possibility of reviving the old parties in the National Front turned out to be illusory. And so KAN Klub—that is, the Club of Committed Nonpartisans—was created. This club did not come out of any clear political tradition; its members had no political experience; it had no leading personalities (where would they have come from anyway?); it was defined primarily in negative terms: none of its members was a communist. For all these reasons, it seemed to me like an organization with a lot of awkward problems. But it was the expression of an authentic and logical social need; it was an attempt to find a solution to one of the biggest social problems of that time.

Why am I talking about this? Even in the Writers' Union, all of whose organs were so far only the formal appendages of certain groups in the party, many writers who had so far been overlooked or unjustifiably pushed aside began to feel the need for a certain—temporary—institutionalization which might make them more effective in defining their own interests, making their demands heard, and being generally dignified partners to party members, not their poor, scattered cousins. From this need arose the Circle of Independent Writers, whose chairman I was elected. That was another way I became involved in the Writers' Union. Before that I'd been

chairman of the Young Authors' Caucus, a slightly wild institution that was created during the struggle over *Tvář*—more
precisely, when most of the young authors, regardless of what
they thought about *Tvář*, understood that defending *Tvář* was
not simply defending a particular magazine; it meant the defense of freedom, which meant their freedom as well. So they
were on our side, there were quite a few of them, and it
seemed that, if they could express their will through a particular kind of association, it might actually lead to some good.
Whether it did or not, I don't know anymore. Perhaps not;
what good it did do was probably indirect—it helped to
change the atmosphere.

As far as 1968 is concerned, I still have vivid memories of
the battles we had when some friends and I, some of them
associated with *Tvář* and some of them "independent," tried
to bring a little fresh air into the Writers' Union and "renew"
it—that was the expression used then. But because the Union
leadership was largely composed of antidogmatic communists, because it published *Literární Noviny,* and because it had
gained a certain amount of credit for itself at the Fourth Congress, it appeared to be one of the more progressive organizations in the country. Therefore, while other organizations
were "renewing" themselves—that is, dropping compromised
people from their leadership—the Writers' Union was not,
and had no intention of doing so, because it seemed renewed
enough as it was. So the credit it enjoyed was in obvious conflict with the way it actually worked: while individual Union
members were speaking at students' meetings alongside the
politicians of the Prague Spring and were thus becoming sym-
bols of the renewal process, the atmosphere inside the Union
remained stale.

I remember, for example, how hard it was to pry Jan Pilař
out of his function as director of the Československý Spisovatel
(The Czechoslovak Writer) publishing house and to put Ladislav
Fikar back (they've had an old-style director back the throne
for many years now). I also remember pleading with Jan
Drda to resign his position on the presidium of the Union; I

told him he was a nice enough man and no one meant him any harm, but his name was a symbol of the Dobříš aristocracy, those writers who had penned, in the Dobříš writers' retreat, their high-flown demands that innocent people can be sentenced to death. I said that if he resigned from that position, at least it would demonstrate that the writing community was prepared to distance itself, once and for all, from its own dark past. I remember Jan Beneš getting ready to read to Ivan Skála and the rest of Skála's article "For Dogs, a Dog's Death," in which Skála had demanded the death sentence for Slánský (whether Beneš actually read it I don't know). I recall the heartrending public confession of Jarmila Glazarová, who had also said some rather unfortunate things during the monster trials of the 1950s. We wanted the writers' organization to come to terms with the terrible way writers had betrayed and dishonored the writer's calling by producing articles that had helped create a climate for mass approval of those show trials, and thus for the executions that followed. That too was a part of my activity in the Writers' Union. I devoted a lot of time to it, but I don't think the time was wasted, either personally or in a general sense.

Antonín Liehm recently told me that his generation had never hungered for power. But isn't it one of that generation's greatest mistakes—this not wanting to hold power? Not knowing, and not wanting to know, that, to put out newspapers and other things on your own terms, you also have to participate in power, that this is a duty, a tax you have to pay? In other words, didn't they voluntarily, in advance, deny themselves power—that is, avoid governing as something improper?

I would like to believe Mr. Liehm when he says that his generation—or, to be more precise, the part of it that shares his attitudes—did not in fact long for power. But I do not believe they were powerless. In their twenties, they were already serving as editors-in-chief and cultural attachés. They were in the personnel departments of universities, deciding which professors could lecture and which could not. When they attacked Seifert, it was entirely possibly that Seifert might have gone to prison, just as Zahradníček had. Which books got published, which plays got performed, which programs would be broadcast on the radio and later on television, and which magazines could be published—it was all in their hands. Is that not power? It was they who created the atmosphere of the time, it was they who, to a considerable extent, decided what could be done and who could do it. They held the fate of countless people directly in their hands. Just because most of them did not end up as political functionaries does not mean that they did not have power.

Nor did their later shift from dogmatism to antidogmatism change very much, because many of them found themselves even higher on the ladder: they became directors of scientific institutions, university professors, directors of theatres and publishing houses and so on. Obviously this brought them into growing conflict with the party bureaucracy, but it was mainly an internal power conflict; and, as a matter of fact, the bureaucracy itself was split in a similar way. How Liehm's comrades and fellow travelers used their power—that is, whether they used it to benefit society or to subjugate it— is a different question. But I would never say they had no power at all, and therefore it makes no sense to say that they were wrong not to want it.

The year 1968 is often mythologized, especially by former communist functionaries. You were one of those who never fell for those grand versions of what happened. How do you remember 1968, and how do you see it today, eighteen years later?

I understand 1968 as the logical outcome and culmination of a long process, lasting for many years, in which, as I say, society gradually became aware of itself and liberated itself; I don't see it just as the clash of two political establishments and the temporary victory of the more liberal one. The rich structuring that took place in society, and the increasing pres-sure of the new social awareness, had to find expression sooner or later in the political sphere. The abyss between life and the system grew deeper.

Still, after the changes that took place in January 1968—like many of my fellow citizens, I suppose, especially those who didn't know what was going on inside the party and were observing all this from the outside—I did not fully realize what was actually opening up here, what was being set in motion. I thought it was just a changing of the guard in high places, and therefore it probably didn't mean very much. So I was all the more surprised by the rapid developments that followed. Of course, everyone was taken by surprise, includ-ing the political leadership. These developments, you see, were not the unambiguous expression of will by the party leadership, or the outcome of a clear program; they were the expression of an excess of pressure in society which found, in the inner party struggle and the political changes that were taking place, an opportunity to blow away the lid that had been trapping it.

It's not true that I didn't succumb to euphoria at all. I think everybody must have been intoxicated and delighted by what was happening. Just think of it. Suddenly you could breathe freely, people could associate freely, fear vanished, taboos were swept away, social conflicts could be openly named and described, a wide variety of interests could be expressed, the mass media once again began to do their proper job, civic self-confidence grew: in short, the ice began to melt and the windows began to open. It would have been hard not to be struck and fascinated by all this! Of course, it's also true that my delight was mixed with increasingly agoniz-ing doubts and hesitations, but I was not alone in this either; it was a general phenomenon.

What caused these doubts and hesitations? In my case, it was primarily knowing how embarrassed the country's leadership was in the face of all these developments. Suddenly these people were enjoying spontaneous support and sympathy, something none of them had ever experienced before, because the only kind of support they had even known was organized from above. Naturally they were pleasantly surprised and even excited by all this. On the other hand, they were afraid of this elemental groundswell of popular good will. Again and again they were caught off guard, because things began to happen and demands began to be made which were sometimes incomprehensible, even terrifying, given how far they overstepped the limits of the "possible" and the "admissable." Let's not forget that these people were all normal party bureaucrats with the right pseudo-education from the party, with all the right illusions and habits and prejudices, with the right curricula vitae, the right social background, and the standard narrow horizon. The only difference was, they were a little more free-thinking and a little more decent than the people whose places they had taken. Now they found themselves immersed in a schizophrenic situation: They both sympathized with and feared the rising expectations in society. They drew support from it without fully understanding it. They wanted it to happen, yet they also wanted to slow it down. They tried to let fresh air in, but they were also wary of it. They wanted reform, but only within the limits of their limited imaginations. The nation, in its euphoria, generously overlooked all this, though it may not have respected them for it.

As a result, the reformers more or less trotted along after developments, rather than providing direction. In itself, this wouldn't have mattered much, because society would ultimately have found a way to sort things out on its own. What was dangerous about the situation was that the leadership, having no clear position on what was happening, had no clear notion of how to face up to it either. Captives of their own illusions, they continually kidded themselves that they could somehow explain all this in private to the Soviets, that the Soviets could be mollified with promises, that society could be kept on a leash, and that in the end the Soviets would have to understand and approve. So they glossed over their differences with the Soviets, closed their eyes to the warning signals, and succumbed to the illusion that they could remain in control of developments. They would let what was still admissable go on, and eliminate what was no longer admissable (they called this the "extremes") in a way acceptable to both the nation and the Kremlin.

The rather hastily prepared new party program—the so-called Action Program brought out in April—faithfully mirrored all these conflicts. It was essentially a patchwork job full of contradictions; it could never have satisfied either the nation or the Kremlin. All of this could be felt in the air with increasing clarity and strength, and therefore the embarrassments and the fears grew all the more agonizing.

Of course, there were other reasons for worry as well, ranging from the unresolved problem of the noncommunist majority (the principle of the leading role of the party was not open to question, and the notion of political plurality was simply beyond the leadership's power to comprehend) to the immovable mass of Stalinists in the security forces and other organs of power. Regardless of how willing people were to admit the possibility of military intervention (and in general they tended not to admit it), they felt it wouldn't be as easy to iron out this whole business with the Kremlin as the leadership seemed to think. The public had fewer illusions about the Soviets than their leaders. The sympathy that the leadership enjoyed—at least in the period I'm talking about now—was tainted by hidden fears that when the crunch came the leadership would back down and betray the national dream.

Did you attend any of the famous public meetings at the time?

I did attend the first and most famous of them, the one that took place in the House of Slavs. It began sometime in the evening, it lasted long into the night, and for the entire time some of the reform communists—Smrkovský, Hejzlar, Švermová, my colleagues Kohout and Procházka, and others—answered questions from the floor. I was sitting in the balcony watching everything with bated breath, and I had some very strange feelings. Primarily, of course, I felt joy: that it was possible to speak so openly, that politicians were talking with anonymous members of the audience, that the truth was being articulated in public. Along with this job, I felt something like satisfaction: suddenly things were being said out loud that I had long thought myself, that I had in fact always known but for the most part had had to keep to myself, and even if I hadn't, I could never have expected them to be understood by those in power.

But I also felt a strange sadness. It was a sadness that came from the spectacle of people who were bound by the ruling ideology clarifying for themselves, after twenty years of rule, things that had been clear to everyone else all through those twenty years. The sadness came from the very reasons for my joy. Even at this stage, the audience still had to correct delicately these "men of January": when they said that the illegalities had begun with the trial of Slánský, the entire hall cried out, "What about Horáková?" And these were mostly young people, who at the time of Horáková's trial were children or had not even yet been born! Why did they—and they especially—have to draw the attention of the most enlightened members of the leading party to their own mistakes? I was also bothered by the easygoing, vaudevillian way the "men of January" tried to outdo each other in witty, epigrammatic replies. Perhaps I was subconsciously afraid that this was a sign of the fatal frivolity with which history is made here. Then again, it may only have been an expression of my own exaggerated sobriety. Later I too was compelled to make speeches in large auditoriums, and I know that, as long as I was able to sway tempestuous audiences toward my own sober and reflective position, it was okay, but I made a pitiful showing beside professionals like Vladimír Škutina or born platform speakers like Luděk Pachman.

During the Prague Spring, did you ever get directly involved in politics?

Not much. I certainly wasn't in any of the centers of action. The reform communists were heading up the political activity, and I was not a reform communist, though by this time I had many friends who were. My main field of activity was the Writers' Union, and we've already talked about that. Besides that, I traveled a lot, since it was one of the few periods in my life when I had a passport. If I remember correctly, my one openly political act at the time was a long article called "On the Theme of an Opposition" which I wrote for *Literární Noviny*. In it, I discussed the possibility of forming a new democratic political party which would be a dignified counterpart to the Communist Party. In other words, the problem of nonparty people all over again! The article attracted considerable attention at the time because, if I'm not mistaken, it was the first (and possibly the last) time that the demand for an opposition party was publicly expressed.

I should say, however, that today I have considerable reservations about that article. I don't believe now that the formation of an opposition party was a realistic idea. Without the traditions, without the experiences, and without the leading personalities, it would have been just as much an exercise in futility as the KAN Klub was. Nor do I think it would have solved any essential problem. As a matter of fact, for some time now I've been skeptical about the very idea of mass political parties (this is surely clear from what I've already said about my own notions of a meaningful organization of society). But what mainly bothers me about that article now is something else. The idea of forming a new political party ought to be proposed by someone who is determined to form such a party—and I was not that person. In those agitated times, I still saw my role as that of a writer who is simply a "witness of his time"; in other words, I had no ambition to become a politician, in the sense of someone who takes on the practical task of organizing a better world. In my own defense, however, I should say that the theme of an opposition party was in the air then; it was talked about everywhere, and many felt that, without real progress toward political plurality, everything would remain only half finished. As a matter of fact, many enlightened communists were appealing to nonparty people to take some step in that direction, with the logical proviso that of course they could not do it themselves. So my article was really an expression of the time and the atmosphere of the time. In any case, the demand for an opposition party is certainly not very unusual; in moments of crisis in communist countries, it regularly and logically surfaces; in Poland, opposition parties are being founded all the time.

I read somewhere that you met personally with leading politicians of that time. Is that correct?

Sometime around the beginning of July, when I came back from one of my trips abroad, I found an invitation on my desk from Premier Černík to attend a meeting of top politicians and writers at the Hrzánský Palace. Of course I went, mainly out of curiosity. It was a nice party that went on long into the night, and there were various goodies to be had. Among the politicians there were Dubček, Černík, Smrkovský, Hájek, Minister of Culture Galuška, and also Husák (he made himself very inconspicuous and didn't say very much; if I'd known at the time that he'd eventually be made first secretary and president, I would certainly have paid more attention to him). Among the writers were Eduard Goldstücker, Jan Procházka, Pavel Kohout, Ludvík Vaculík, Josef Škvorecký, myself, and someone else I can't remember now.

I have vivid memories of this encounter, particularly because it was the only time in my life that I have ever had the chance to talk personally with politicians in power (of course, I've been in frequent contact since then with politicians who lost power). At first I was shy, but after bolstering my courage with a cognac, I got into a long conversation with Dubček. As I recall it, I eagerly explained all kinds of things to him, and with great self-assurance advised him about how to avoid Soviet intervention and cut people like Indra off from power (at the time, Indra was sending out some very suspicious telexes behind the backs of the leadership). I advised him to allow the Social Democrats to come back and not to cause difficulties for the former political prisoners in the K-231 Club; I told him he should get rid of any illusions about the Kremlin, that he shouldn't always be on the defensive and trying to pacify public opinion in the hope that it would somehow help; and so on. Thanks to the cognac, I behaved rather impertinently, and much of what I told him was no doubt nonsense, but there is one thing I will never forget: for the entire time, Dubček listened very intently, and he even asked a few supplementary questions. Of course he didn't follow much of my advice, but the fact that he talked to me at all won me over. This kind of thing is not at all common among politicians, especially communists, because they are too busy churning out their own phrases and clichés to listen to anyone.

Do you think that there was any real way of getting out of that crisis? Of avoiding an invasion? Do you think that we might have, or should have, defended ourselves?

As we know, the "what ifs" of history are very misleading. There's a queer tradition in this country that after every historical screw-up a thousand and one clever people suddenly appear who know precisely what we should have done and claim that the outcome would have been quite different had we behaved in such-and-such a way. But since you ask, I will try to answer your question.

In the first place, I have to say that I find all the bluster about how we should have fought back very suspect; often it's simply compensation for some odd feelings of inferiority. Theoretically, perhaps, some symbolic act of defense might have been possible. For instance, I've heard—and I don't know to what extent it's true—that Prague's anti-aircraft defenses could have held off the Soviet air force for at least three days. But I don't think any organized defense of this kind was possible at all. In order for that to happen, all the mobilization and battle plans would have had to be completely redone and turned in the opposite direction. But of course, as soon as anyone started doing that, the Soviets would have been here, because the entire Czechoslovak high command is riddled with Soviet agents, and the slightest whisper there is known to the general secretary of the Soviet Union before it is known to the Czechoslovak president.

A modern army is an enormous machine, and it can't simply be given an order to go here or there. For decades now, our army has been a satellite army. Apart from a single timid remark by General Prchlík about the possibility of decentralizing the Warsaw Pact, for which he was immediately required to resign, nothing at all was done during the entire renewal process (and, given its nature, nothing could have been done) to make our army more independent. So the notion that someone should have ordered the army to defend the country in August 1968 is rather naïve. And in any case who would have given such an order? The leadership would have had to be completely different. Where would such a leadership have come from? And if there had been a different leadership, events before August would have unfolded differently, in which case who can tell what the situation in August would have been?

As you see, these "what ifs" really are misleading. The spontaneous resistance of some units and garrisons might have been a more realistic possibility, and there are indica-

tions that some of the enlisted men and lower-ranking officers would have had the courage to do this. But, again,
something like that could only have happened in a moral and
political atmosphere very different from the kind that dominated the country before August. In other words, one "what
if" leads to another. But even if military resistance had been
militarily feasible and politically realistic, its consequences
would have been difficult to imagine. The easiest to imagine—insignificant historically but important from the point
of view of our conversation—would be my absence from this
world, or at least my absence from any other place on it except Siberia.

*But, on the other hand, to simplify considerably, the dead
would probably not have allowed the living to make compromises and pacts so quickly with the occupiers. It might
even have straightened our spines. And we should probably
also remind ourselves that freedom is never granted, it must
be fought for and usually paid for in blood—*

I would be very, very careful about making speculations
of that kind. If people are willing, in extreme situations, to
shed their own blood for freedom, they have a greater chance
of actually gaining that freedom than if they are not willing
to do so; to that extent I agree with you. But I would immediately add another important thing: such decisions cannot
be made for others. If you wish to sacrifice your life for our
common freedom, you may. If I wish to sacrifice my life, I
may. But neither you nor I have any right to compel anyone
else to do it, or not to ask him and simply to sacrifice his life.
If I were a military commander who could give the order for
anti-aircraft batteries to defend Prague, I would probably only
do so if I could be persuaded that an overwhelming majority
of Czechoslovaks were determined to bear the probable consequences of my order, including death in an Afghan type of
massacre.

Does this mean you think the occupation and the defeat couldn't have been prevented?

I'm not saying that. But I definitely don't think the occupation could have been prevented while preserving something more important by exercising greater control over the social processes that were going on, by defusing the popular will, by liquidating the so-called extremes, by discipline, by censorship, and by compromises. The only meaningful way, it seems to me, would have been for the leadership to jump into the current, to ride it, identify with it, and use its energy in all sorts of ways to defend it. The way was not continually to hide things, conceal them, extinguish them, gloss them over. In my opinion, the leadership should not have behaved like a guilty servant; on the contrary, they should have tried to extract the maximum potential from the situation that arose. Often to their own surprise, people began to feel civic and national confidence; they began to feel proud and autonomous. If the leadership had also behaved with pride and autonomy, they would have had this enormous background of support in society. There was a real opportunity here for a moral mobilization; the leadership could have drawn on this renewed sense of national confidence, and systematically encouraged and strengthened it. After all, Tito and Ceausescu did this for years when they were trying to forestall a Soviet invasion. It would have been enough to emphasize continually that we would not surrender, that we stood by our positions, that we would not allow a single foreign soldier to cross our borders. A civilian home guard could have been set up, and it might even have been possible to carry out some kind of military mobilization outside the Warsaw Pact maneuvers calendar (remember the political impact that the May mobilization had in 1938). The Kremlin leadership undertook the invasion only because it knew there would be no military resistance here. Even the aging Brezhnev leadership would have been rational enough not to risk a new Vietnam in the middle of a Europe that was armed to the teeth. Perhaps all we had to do was create uncertainty in the Kremlin—that is, constantly and stubbornly to generate an atmosphere in which there was an increasing national will to defend our independence, and not rule out in advance the possibility that some army units might spontaneously fight to defend the country. The leadership directly fed into the much-feared extremes by its own hesitancy, by its inability to say either A or B; if it had clearly stood behind the social process, perhaps there wouldn't have been so many extremes, and their potential would have been diverted from a need to deal constantly with the latent mistrust toward those in power, to an active and loyal support for the interests of the whole society. In other words, if the leadership had made intelligent use of the capital it had at its disposal, it might have been able to create a situation in which the Soviets would have had to think very seriously indeed about military intervention of any kind.

While appealing to national awareness and confidence, however, the leaders would also have had to seek support and solidarity internationally—not directly, in the form of military agreements, since there was no one to make them with anyway, but as part of a broad attempt to popularize Czechoslovak themes as European themes. They would have had, somehow, to make others generally aware that our emancipation was an unequivocally positive phenomenon, that it would not destabilize the European status quo but would, on the contrary, contribute to a genuinely peaceful order founded on overcoming the bloc mentality and on the notion of a plurality of autonomous European nations.

We don't know, and will probably never know, whether such a policy would have worked, but I can't help feeling that it might have been more successful than what was tried. If the partisans of intervention in the Soviet Politburo had been outvoted, developments there too might have been accelerated, but in any case it would have meant that the Soviets were prepared to negotiate seriously, and make some concessions. We would obviously have had to make some concessions ourselves; unfortunately, that's the way things work in politics. But it needn't have turned out as catastrophically as it did. The Soviets are not impressed by abject apologies: that is just grist to their mill. What works with them is taking a firm stand. But can people who are full of illusions take a firm stand? Not very likely. Once again we're faced with one of those misleading historical "what ifs." To be more concrete, remember how powerfully both the Soviets and the Czechoslovak public were affected when our politicians refused to go to that meeting in Dresden and replied to the letter from Dresden with one of their own. That moment had an absolutely cathartic moral significance; if, instead of being the last proud act ever made by the Communist Party of Czechoslovakia, it had been the first of many such acts, such as banning Warsaw Pact maneuvers on Czechoslovak territory, perhaps things would have turned out better; it's always easier to attack someone who is retreating.

However it might have been, by the time August came around not much was salvageable, and the sad and perhaps even tragic thing is that, from society's point of view, it was extremely fortunate that our leadership was so clumsily straitjacketed and taken off to Moscow. On the one hand, this had a lot to do with stimulating the popular, nonviolent resistance to the occupation, and, on the other hand, through the silencing of the indecisive party leadership, the main obstacle to a genuinely authentic manifestation of the social will was temporarily eliminated. And that will was entirely positive and creative—in other words, not "extreme" at all! It was a belated manifestation of a political capital that should have been recognized and made use of long before that.

What about the Moscow agreements?

It's all part of the same problem: what else could you expect? Of course, they could have—following Kriegel's example—not signed anything, dug in their heels, and demanded that the negotiations be broken off to give the delegation a chance to consult with its own representative organs and with the people. They could have stressed that a delegation so constituted had not been sent or authorized by any recognized Czechoslovak body, and that therefore they could sign nothing, and that in any case, without knowing what the situation was at home, they certainly could not sign anything.

Instead of behaving like the proud representatives of a sovereign country, they behaved like guilty servants. After the Soviets had taken their handcuffs off and turned them into an official state-and-party delegation before the eyes of the entire world, it would have been very difficult for them to be put back into their straitjackets. But even if that were not possible, it seems to me our representatives had a responsibility to take the risk. The Soviets, after all, were in a very precarious situation. Let's not forget the immense importance of prestige in all their political actions, and this could certainly have been used to play for time, to allow the pathos of the situation to deepen, to wait for the Soviets to make concessions (and concessions would have had to come sooner or later, even if only in the form of recognizing the extraordinary Vysočany Congress). Whether all of that would have led to something concrete I don't know; perhaps its effect would "only" have been moral and symbolic. Nevertheless, even that might have had a real impact. At the very least, the disintegration that took place here after the occupation would have proceeded more slowly.

August 21 found you in North Bohemia. What did you do during those first hectic days of the occupation?

That night I happened to be in Liberec with my wife and Jan Tříska; we were staying with friends, and we remained for that whole dramatic week, because our friends brought us into the Liberec resistance, if I can call it that. We worked in the broadcasting station there. I wrote a commentary every day, Honza read them on the air, and we even appeared on television, in a studio that was rigged up on Ještěd [a high hill where there is a T.V. station and transmitter]. We were also part of the National Committee chairman's permanent staff; we helped coordinate various activities; I wrote speeches for the chairman, and I even wrote lengthy declarations for the District Committee of the Communist Party, the District National Committee, the District Committee of the National Front, the town National Committee, and so on, which were then broadcast to the population over the street loudspeakers and pasted up everywhere on the walls. I think that was the first and last time I ever had the opportunity to speak to the nation through the mouths of such august institutions.

That week was an experience I'll never forget. I saw Soviet tanks smash down arcades on the main square and bury several people in the rubble. I saw a tank commander start shooting wildly into the crowd. I saw and experienced many things, but what affected me most powerfully was that special phenomenon of solidarity and community which was so typical of that time. People would bring food and flowers and medicine to the radio station, regardless of whether we needed them or not. When Tříska didn't broadcast for a couple of hours, the station was bombarded with telephone calls asking if we were all right. The radio building was ringed with huge transport trucks loaded down with large cement blocks to prevent us from being taken over. Factories sent us passes that would enable us to conceal ourselves among the workers if we found ourselves in any personal danger.

Clearly, because of the bloody events I've mentioned, Liberec was not occupied by a Soviet garrison for that whole period; the troops simply passed through it. This was also why the spontaneous popular resistance in Liberec was able to grow to greater dimensions, and assume more forms, than it could in towns and cities that were occupied. Antioccupation folklore soon turned the town into a single enormous artifact. There were endless ideas on how to foil the occupation. And things were never more efficient than they were then. The

print shop could put out a book in two days, and all kinds of
enterprises were able to do almost anything right away. I remember a typical story: The scourge of Liberec and environs
was a gang of about a hundred tough young men called
"Tramps" who would go on weekend forays into the country-
side. For a long time, the town officials hadn't been able to
put a stop to them. The leader was a fellow they called the
Pastor. Shortly after the invasion, the Pastor showed up at the
chairman's office in the town hall and said, "I'm at your disposal, chief." The chairman was somewhat nonplussed, but
he decided to give the gang a trial job: "All right," he said,
"tonight I want you to take down all the street signs, so the
occupiers can't find their way around. It's not appropriate to
have the police do that." The Pastor nodded, and the next
morning all the street signs in Liberec were neatly stacked in
front of the town-hall steps. Not a single one had been dam-
aged. And there they stayed until they could be put up again.
The Pastor then asked for another job. And thus arose a
strange collaboration, one result of which was that for two
days members of the Pastor's gang wore armbands of the aux-
iliary guard, and three-man patrols walked through the town:
a uniformed policeman in the middle with two long-haired
Tramps on either side. This gang also did twenty-four-hour
sentry duty at the town hall. They guarded the mayor, and
checked everyone who entered the building. There were some
poignant scenes: for instance, the whole town-hall staircase
was packed with these fellows on duty, playing their guitars
and singing "Massachusetts," which was a kind of world an-
them for hippies then. I saw the whole thing in a special light,
because I still had fresh memories of crowds of similar young
people in the East Village in New York, singing the same
song, but without the tanks in the background.

I'm not one of those who somehow got mentally stuck in
that week of occupation and have then spent the rest of their
lives reminiscing about what it was like. And I have no intention of romanticizing that period either. I only think that,
taken all together, it made for a unique phenomenon which

to this day, as far as I know, has never been analyzed in any depth sociologically, philosophically, psychologically, or politically. But some things were so obvious you could understand them immediately, without any scientific analysis. For example, that society is a very mysterious animal with many faces and hidden potentialities, and that it's extremely short-sighted to believe that the face society happens to be presenting to you at a given moment is its only true face. None of us know all the potentialities that slumber in the spirit of the population, or all the ways in which that population can surprise us when there is the right interplay of events, both visible and invisible. Who would have believed—at a time when the Novotný regime was corroding away because the entire nation was behaving like Švejks—that half a year later that same society would display a genuine civic-mindedness, and that a year later this recently apathetic, skeptical, and demoralized society would stand up with such courage and intelligence to a foreign power! And who would have suspected that, after scarcely a year had gone by, this same society would, as swiftly as the wind blows, lapse back into a state of demoralization far deeper than its original one! After all these experiences, one must be very careful about coming to any conclusions about the way we are, or what can be expected of us.

Something else: that week showed how helpless military power is when confronted by an opponent unlike any that power has been trained to confront; it showed how hard it is to govern a country in which, though it may not defend itself militarily, all the civil structures simply turn their backs on the aggressors. And this is not to mention things like the principal and as yet unrecognized significance of the modern media as a political power in their own right, capable of directing and coordinating all social life. That week in August is a historical experience that cannot be wiped out of the awareness of our nations, though we can't say yet what it really meant, or what marks it has left on the genetic material of society, and how and when these will manifest themselves.

*How do you see the stormy period at the end of 1968 and in
early 1969? What were you doing then, and how did you
experience that period?*

It was a strange and tortured time. As I've already said, I
didn't take much part in public life before August. The whirl-
wind the occupation left in its wake drew me into it. The
leadership made concession after concession in the hopes of
salvaging something, but all it did was saw off the very limb
it was sitting on. Gradually, unstoppably, the old forms of
order were reconstituted, but it was still possible to speak and
write freely. That was what made the time seem so tortured:
Things were said openly, in tough language, but all we could
really talk about was our own helplessness. There were energetic protests, but all we could really protest about was the
fact that our protests were being ignored. It was a time of big
student strikes, endless meetings, petitions, negotiations,
demonstrations, and passionate debates. The ship was slowly
going under, and the passengers were allowed to shout that
this was happening. Palach's death, which at any other time
would have been difficult to understand, was understood immediately by the whole society, because it was an extreme and
almost symbolic expression of the "spirit of the time": everyone knew that desperate need to do something desperately
extreme when everything else failed, for everyone carried such
a need within himself.

At the time, I took part in everything I could; it was simply
impossible not to. I took part in debates in universities and
factories, I took part in meetings, I wrote declarations, and I
felt I had to be involved in all of this (for example, I turned
down the chance to study for a month in Italy in the foolish
belief that I was needed here; but many people felt the same
way). I stressed, perhaps somewhat more energetically than
others, that every concession gives rise to further concessions,
that we cannot back down, because behind us there is only
an abyss, that we must keep our promises and demand that
they be kept. I struggled, as was my habit, against all kinds of

illusions and every form of self-deception. However influenced I might have been by that agitated period, I tried to achieve a soberness and a balance. In the spirit of the old *Tvář* approach—although with obvious differences, for this was a different level of activity, after all—I opposed to every grandiose but vague demand the need simply to remain steadfast to the end in matters that were smaller, perhaps, but more concrete.

At one large meeting of the central committees of all the artistic unions, a well-known actor (the same one who a few years later, during the hue and cry against Charter 77, went on television to spit on a former friend of his who had signed the Charter) made a dramatic appeal for the establishment of a national tribunal to try Indra, Bilǎk, and other traitors of the nation. Hysterical nonsense. I got up immediately and replied that, instead of suggesting something that no one could ever hope to carry off, it would be better to attempt something possible, something within our power, such as sticking by the solidarity agreement that every cultural worker had signed (and which was shortly after that betrayed by most of them). I said it was a thousand times more valuable to insist, regardless of the consequences, on something more modest but realistic, than to pacify one's conscience by firing off loudmouthed proposals that evaporate forever the moment they're made and therefore commit no one to do anything about them. Histrionic emotions expressed through proposals like that are extremely unreliable: they may be grand today, but the resignation felt tomorrow can be equally as great (something the actor, this avenger of the nation, demonstrated marvelously). Sober perseverance is more effective than enthusiastic emotions, which are all too capable of being transferred, with little difficulty, to something different each day.

Since we're talking about this period, I'd like to mention a small story of my own. Materially it's insignificant, but to me it's highly symbolic. Later, under Husák now, there was another general assembly of the central committees of the creative unions; this was clearly going to be the last such assembly, because the unions were shortly going to be reconstituted or simply dissolved and replaced by new unions set up by a handful of selected people. Since we knew we were all here together for the last time, the idea came up that we should write and sign something like a last will and testament to the nation, a kind of manifesto in which we would swear never to give up our truth no matter what happened. It was going to be a binding document, suggestively written, perhaps even historical. I was named to a three-member committee in charge of producing a quick draft, and we retired to a small room in the film club to write it. Unfortunately, I was also expected to participate in the opening of a show of paintings by a friend of mine in the Spálená Gallery, on Spálená Street, not far away. I wasn't going to give a serious speech—there were art historians for that—just take part in a little program of verses and songs. This was the dadaist wish of my friend, who loved the way I sang patriotic songs out of tune and gave impassioned recitations from our national literary classics at parties. And so, pretending that I had to go to the bathroom, I fled from the task of writing the historic manifesto and I ran to the gallery opening, where I sang and recited to a shocked audience, then rushed back to the film club to write the final paragraph.

The manifesto was unanimously approved by the plenary session; everyone signed it; and almost no one lived up to it. But that's not why I'm talking about these things; I have another reason. There is something symbolic in this accidental juxtaposition of writing a serious manifesto and giving an absurd performance at an art-show opening, something that is a comment not only on the specific climate of those turbulent and paradoxical times and my position in them, but on the general climate in Prague, Bohemia, and Central Europe. For isn't it characteristic that the miserable historical events we are condemned to live through, in which we try to do our best at a cost that is all but incomprehensible elsewhere, are organically wedded here to our traditional sense of irony and self-deprecation, to our sense of the absurd, to our own free or black sense of humor? Don't these two things somehow belong essentially together? Don't they condition each other? Isn't it entirely possible that we would not be able to carry out our historic role and make the sacrifices that are required of us if we could not maintain this constant distance from them and from ourselves? So not only does the one not exclude the other, it's as if each pole made the other one possible!

Foreigners are sometimes amazed at the suffering that we are willing to undergo here, and at the same time they are amazed at the things we are still able to laugh at. It's difficult to explain, but without the laughter we would simply be unable to do the serious things. If one were required to increase the dramatic seriousness of his face in relation to the seriousness of the problems he had to confront, he would quickly petrify and become his own statue. And such a statue could scarcely write another historical manifesto or be equal to any human task! If you don't want to dissolve in your own seriousness to the point where you become ridiculous to everyone, you must have a healthy awareness of your own human ridiculousness and nothingness. As a matter of fact, the more serious what you are doing is, the more important it becomes not to lose this awareness. If you lose this, your own actions—paradoxically—lose their own seriousness. A human action becomes genuinely important when it springs from the soil of a clearsighted awareness of the temporality and the ephemerality of everything human. It is only this awareness that can breathe any greatness into an action. The outlines of genuine meaning can only be perceived from the bottom of absurdity. Everything else is superficial, and just as ephemeral as that proposal to set up a tribunal to try Bilăk.

I would even claim that, in the seventeen years that separate me from that manifesto, I have not really betrayed it to any great extent. And this was not despite the fact that during the writing of it I took time off to play the clown; on the contrary, it may have been precisely because of that! And because I'm continually "taking time off."

People often ask me how my "preposterous idealism" goes along with the fact that I write absurd plays. I reply that they are only two sides of the same coin. Without the constantly living and articulated experience of absurdity, there would be no reason to attempt to do something meaningful. And, on the contrary, how can one experience one's own absurdity if one is not constantly seeking meaning? But I've got a little bit off the topic, haven't I?

It doesn't matter, I'll bring you back to the facts. In August 1969, at the very end of the period we're talking about, you apparently wrote a private letter to Alexander Dubček. Why did you write him, and what was the letter about?

That was the time when everyone was waiting anxiously to see how Dubček would behave. Would he carry out some kind of self-criticism or, on the contrary, would he have the nerve to analyze the situation truthfully and thus bring his brief era to a dignified end? At the time, I was afraid that Dubček, out of an impersonal loyalty to the party and an attempt not to "get in the way," would somehow spoil this opportunity, so I wrote him a long letter in which I explained to him from all possible points of view how important it was for the nation, for the future, for history, and even for socialism that he not lose his proper face, precisely now, when he was being more or less consigned to the trash heap.

I know that he got the letter; I don't know what he thought of it. He disappeared rather quietly and inconspicuously from political life; he didn't betray his own cause by renouncing it, but he didn't bring his political career to a very vivid end either. Not long ago I came across a copy of that letter, which I'd long since forgotten, and as I read it seventeen years later, one passage caught my attention more than any other: I had written that even a purely moral act that has no hope of any immediate and visible political effect can gradually and indirectly, over time, gain in political significance. In this I found, to my own surprise, the very same idea that, having been discovered by many people at the same time, stood behind the birth of Charter 77 and which to this day I am trying—in relation to the Charter and our "dissident activities"—to develop and explain and, in various ways, make more precise.

IV

Public Enemy

If you were to have to describe the 1970s in Czechoslovakia, what would you say about them? What was your experience of that period—say from 1970 until the time of your third arrest, in 1979?

John Lennon once said that the 1970s weren't worth a damn. And, indeed, when we look back on them today—I'm thinking now in the world context—they seem, compared with the rich and productive 1960s, to be lacking in significance, style, atmosphere, with no vivid spiritual and cultural movements. The seventies were bland, boring, and bleak. For me they are symbolized on the one hand by Leonid Brezhnev and his stuffy rule, and on the other hand by the ambiguous figure of President Nixon, with his strange war in Vietnam and its strange end, and the absurd Watergate affair.

In Czechoslovakia, the seventies were perhaps even gloomier. After the Soviet intervention and its rather caustic aftermath, Husák replaced Dubček, and a long period of moribund silence began. A new ruling elite, which was in fact much like the old one, quickly formed and carried out all those purges, prohibitions, and liquidations. An exhausted society quickly got used to the fact that everything once declared forever impossible was now possible again, and that an often unmasked and ridiculed absurdity could rule once more. People withdrew into themselves and stopped taking an interest in public affairs. An era of apathy and widespread demoralization began, an era of gray, everyday totalitarian consumerism. Society was atomized, small islands of resistance were destroyed, and a disappointed and exhausted public pretended not to notice. Independent thinking and creation retreated to the trenches of deep privacy.

For me, the first half of the decade is a single, shapeless fog; I can't say any longer how 1972, for instance, differed from 1973, or what I did in either of those years. Like most of my colleagues, I was driven out of every position I'd once held, I was publicly branded an enemy, and I was even indicted for subversion (there was no trial or prison sentence). Ultimately, I too had no choice but to withdraw into a kind of internal exile. My wife and I spent most of our time at Hrádeček, our cottage in the Krkonoše Mountains, which we gradually adapted and renovated. I tortured myself writing *The Conspirators,* the first play I wrote as a banned writer; after the excitement and stimulation of the years before, no play took me longer or was harder to write, and it's clearly the weakest of my plays. I once compared it to a chicken that had been in the oven for too long and completely dried out. Of course, no one was waiting for the play or pressing me to finish it, so it really was written in a kind of vacuum. As I worked on it, I spent too much time wondering how to come to terms with the completely new situation both in society and for myself personally, and, inevitably, almost all the life was squeezed out of it.

The only thing that disturbed the public waters, at least in the milieu in which I moved, was a writer's petition in defense of political prisoners; I'll come back to that later. At the beginning of the 1970s, I became close with some colleagues whom fate had dealt a similar blow. These were former communists, people I've referred to as "antidogmatics" who in earlier days had often been my opponents. Each summer, Pavel Kohout, Ludvík Vaculík, Ivan Klíma, Jan Trefulka, and others would come to our cottage, where we held our own miniature writers' congresses. Of course, another group would come along every summer as well, friends from earlier times, noncommunist writers I'd known back in the 1950s, when I was their "apprentice," some of whom were with me in *Tvář* and later belonged to our Circle of Independent Writ-

ers. In this group were people like Zdeněk Urbanek, Jan Vladislav, Josef Hiršal, Josef Vohryzek, Ladislav Dvořák, Petr
Kopta, and occasionally (with one or the other of those
groups) came writers like Jiří Gruša, Alexandr Kliment, Milan
Uhde, Petr Kabeš, Karel Sidon, Josef Topol, and once even
Václav Černý took part; Jiří Kolář wanted to come but never
actually made it.

These two groups gradually "fused"; they would come together or mingle in various ways, which was a rather symptomatic phenomenon: these people all had very different
pasts, but the differences of opinion that had once separated
them had long since ceased to be important. We were all in
the same boat and we were in agreement about general matters. The tradition that was established then developed in various ways, and in fact has continued to this day in another
form. During these encounters, we read each other our next
texts.

Apart from that, however, we were quite isolated, and the
popular term "ghetto" seems to me the most adequate to describe that period. The public of course knew us well, and
were aware of us and sympathized with us, but at the same
time they were careful not to have anything to do with us:
it seemed too dangerous. And in this period of general atom-
ization or disintegration, we didn't have very good contacts with other groups or circles either. Each of us, in his
own way, was stewing in his own juices. Having been marked
in a particular fashion, with no hope for any kind of wider
support, we had no way of actively expressing ourselves,
so for the most part we passively accepted our situation and
simply wrote. At that time, there were regular readings of new
texts at Ivan Klíma's place. Quite a few people attended,
and I myself read two plays there, *The Conspirators* and, a
year later, *The Beggar's Opera*. We also followed each other's
work in written form. The texts were copied out and circulated, which is how the now famous Edice Petlice came into
being (its younger sister, Edice Expedice was created in
1975).

In 1974 I was employed for about ten months as a worker in the Trutnov Brewery, about ten kilometers from Hrádeček. In a conversation with Jiří Lederer in 1975, I said I had gone to work there for financial reasons, but, looking back now, I think the real reason was that I needed a change. The suffocating inactivity all around me was beginning to get on my nerves. I wanted to get out of my shelter for a while and take a look around, be among different people.

One of the things that contributed—somewhat paradoxically—to the gloom of the time was the fact that this was also a period of détente. In our case, this meant that many of our Western friends and collaborators avoided us almost as circumspectly as official writers here did, so they wouldn't annoy the authorities and frustrate attempts at rapprochement with those authorities. Fortunately, this naïve, thickheaded, and suicidal way of "easing tensions" is not practiced by many people from the West anymore, with the exception, perhaps, of a few West German Social Democrats.

For me personally, the first noticeable break in the long and boring sentence of the 1970s was 1975. There were three reasons for this. First, the idea that it was time to stop being merely a passive object of those "victories written by history," as Václav Bělohradský calls them, and to try to become their subject for a moment. In other words, it was time to stop waiting to see what "they" would do and do something myself, compel *them* for a change to deal with something they hadn't counted on. So I wrote a long open letter to Husák. In it, I tried to analyze the sad situation in our country; to point to the profound spiritual, moral, and social crisis hidden behind the apparent tranquility of social life. I urged Husák to realize just how much he himself was responsible for this general misery.

I have vivid memories of that letter, and it was because of that that I visited you at Hrádeček.

I remember that. The letter, on the primary level, was a kind of autotherapy: I had no idea what would happen next, but it was worth the risk. I regained my balance and my self-confidence. I felt I could stand up straight again, and that no one could accuse me any longer of not doing anything, of just looking on in silence at the miserable state of affairs. I could breathe more easily because I had not tried to stifle the truth inside me. I had stopped waiting for the world to improve and exercised my right to intervene in that world, or at least to express my opinion about it. At the same time, it had a wider significance: it was one of the first coherent— and generally comprehensible—critical voices to be heard here, and a general response was not long in coming. Obviously I had hit a moment when all this endless waiting around had begun to get on a lot of people's nerves, people who were tired of their own exhaustion, and had begun to recover from that roundhouse right. So people copied my letter out and passed it on, and it was read by practically everyone who still cared. Naturally I was enormously pleased and encouraged by this response.

The second important event of that year for me was writing my one-act play *Audience*. It was inspired by my time in the brewery, and it was the first appearance of Vaněk, the writer. I wrote it quickly, in a couple of days, originally just to amuse friends to whom I wanted to read it during our summer sessions at Hrádeček. To my surprise, there was a wonderful response to that play too, and in time it actually became popular, in the literal sense of the word. Not only did it play—along with the subsequent Vaněk one-acters—in theatres of all sorts in the rest of the world; what was, understandably, more important for me was that the play entered people's awareness at home—first of all as a written text, and later as performed by my friend Pavel Landovský and me on a tape that was later released as a record by Šafrán in Sweden. Things began to happen to me. For example, I once picked up a hitchhiker and, without knowing who I was, he began to quote passages from that play. Or I'd be sitting in a pub and I'd hear young people shouting lines from the play to each other across the room. That too was very encouraging, not only because it was a flattering reminder of happier days, when my plays were being performed, when it was almost a cultural duty to know them, but above all because it suggested to me that even a playwright who is cut off from his theatre can still have an impact on his own domestic milieu. He is still an integral part of it.

The third important experience in 1975 was the perfor-mance of my play *The Beggar's Opera* in Horní Počernice. The play is a free adaptation of John Gay's old play, and has noth-ing to do with Brecht at all. I originally wrote the play at the request of a Prague theatre that wanted to perform it under someone else's name, but that offer fell through. My old friend Andrej Krob, who had once collaborated with us at the The-atre on the Balustrade, rehearsed the play with an amateur group of friends, young students, and workers who liked the play and decided that they would rehearse it regardless of the fact that I was under a very strict ban. So they rehearsed it and then they performed it—only once, naturally—in a res-taurant called U Čelikovských in Horní Počernice. Right up to the very last minute, I didn't think the performance would actually take place. But it did, thanks mainly to the inatten-tion of the local authorities, who thought the title sounded familiar and so allowed it to go on without making any fur-ther inquiries about who'd written it. Knowing that it would be an unrepeatable event, we invited everyone we could think of to come. There were about three hundred friends and ac-quaintances in the audience. Today, when I look at the pho-tographs of the audience, I can see several future spokesmen for Charter 77, countless future signatories, but also actors and directors from the Prague theatres and other persons in cultural life.

The performance was marvelous; the laughter and de-light of the audience seemed endless, and for a moment I was back again in the atmosphere of the Theatre on the Balustrade in the 1960s. Thanks to the circumstances, it was, understandably, even more exciting. The matter-of-factness with which these young people acted in my play gave their performance a special theatrical charm. It was a human act that had somehow, miraculously, been transformed into a highly suggestive theatrical act. At the party after the performance (and, by the way, this was right under the lamppost, at the restaurant U Medvídku, just around the corner from police headquarters on Bartolomějská Street in Prague), I told the troupe that I had more joy from this premiere than from all my foreign premieres, from New York to Tokyo.

The consequences were not long in coming. There was a huge to-do about it, and the matter was taken up by all kinds of institutions. There were interrogations and sanctions; enraged bureaucrats spread the word through the official Prague theatres that because of me (!) the cultural policy of the government would be that much more stringent, and the whole theatre community would suffer. Many a shallow-minded actor fell for it and got very upset at me and my amateur actors for frustrating their artistic ambition, by which, of course, they meant their well-paid sprints from job to job—in dubbing, theatre, television, and film—that is, from one center for befuddling the public to another. But that wasn't the point. For me the most important thing was that, for the first time in seven years (and the only time in the next eleven to follow), I had seen a play of mine on the stage, and I could see with my own eyes that I was still capable of writing something that could be performed. All these events made me feel I had something left in me, and gave me energy for further enterprises.

Do you feel like reminiscing about the prehistory and the origin of Charter 77?

For me personally, it all began sometime in January or February 1976. I was at Hrádeček, alone, there was snow everywhere, a night blizzard was raging outside, I was writing something, and suddenly there was a pounding on the door. I opened it, and there stood a friend of mine, whom I don't wish to name, half frozen and covered with snow. We spent the night discussing things over a bottle of cognac he'd brought with him. Almost as an aside, this friend suggested that I meet Ivan Jirous, and he even offered to set up a meeting, because he saw him frequently. I already knew Jirous; I'd met him about twice in the late 1960s, but I hadn't seen him since then. Occasionally I would hear wild and, as I discovered later, quite distorted stories about the group of people that had gathered around him, which he called the underground, and about the Plastic People of the Universe, a nonconformist rock group that was at the center of this society; Jirous was their artistic director.

I understood from my friend the snowman that Jirous' opinion of me was not exactly flattering either: he apparently saw me as a member of the official, and officially tolerated, opposition—in other words, a member of the establishment. But a month later, when I was in Prague, thanks to my friend the snowman, I actually did meet Jirous. His hair was down to his shoulders, other long-haired people would come and go, and he talked and talked and told me how things were. He gave me his "Report on the Third Czech Musical Revival" and he played me songs by the Plastic People, DG 307, and other Czech underground groups on a rasping old tape recorder. Although I'm no expert on rock music, I immediately felt that there was something rather special radiating from these performances, that they were not just deliberately oddball or dilettantish attempts to be outlandish at any price, as what I had heard about them before might have suggested; the music was a profoundly authentic expression of the sense of life among these people, battered as they were by the misery of this world. There was disturbing magic in the music, and a kind of inner warning. Here was something serious and genuine, an internally free articulation of an existential experience that everyone who had not become completely obtuse must understand.

Jirous' own explanations quickly dispelled the doubts I had harbored from the fragmentary and sometimes derisory accounts I'd heard before. Suddenly I realized that, regardless of how many vulgar words these people used or how long their hair was, truth was on their side. Somewhere in the midst of this group, their attitudes, and their creations, I sensed a special purity, a shame, and a vulnerability; in their music was an experience of metaphysical sorrow and a longing for salvation. It seemed to me that this underground of Jirous' was an attempt to give hope to those who had been most excluded. I was already very late for a party at Pavel Kohout's place, and I telephoned to apologize; Pavel was annoyed, but I couldn't very well explain over the phone why talking to Jirous was more important to me at that moment. Jirous and I went on to a pub, and we carried on almost until morning. He invited me to a concert that was supposed to take place about two weeks later somewhere just outside Prague, but the concert never took place: in the meantime, the authorities arrested Jirous and his band, along with some other singers in the underground, a total of about nineteen people.

I was at Hrádeček when I learned about this, and I came to Prague immediately, since it was obvious that something had to be done, and equally obvious that it was up to me to do it. I also knew it wouldn't be easy to gain some kind of wider support for these boys. Among the people who might have helped, almost no one knew them, and those who did, harbored similar doubts to those I had felt before meeting Magor (that is Jirous' nickname). I had almost nothing concrete to prove that they weren't the layabouts, hooligans, alcoholics, and drug addicts that the regime was portraying them as in the hopes of being able simply to sweep them out of the way.

At the same time, I felt we had to do something not only

on principle—because something ought to be done when someone is unjustly arrested—but also because of the special significance this case seemed to have, a meaning that seemed to transcend the details. Political prisoners from the early 1970s were gradually returning from prison. The high sentences they received had been an act of political revenge: the regime understood these people, correctly, as an opposition; it knew they would not surrender, so it settled its accounts with them as vanquished enemies who refused to behave as such. Their trials were essentially the last political trials for several years; everything seemed to indicate that prison would remain an extreme threat and that those in power had actually succeeded in developing more sophisticated ways of manipulating society. People had become somewhat used to this by now, and they were all the more inclined to treat the case of the Plastic People as a genuinely criminal affair. At the same time, this confrontation was, in its own way, more serious and more dangerous than those trials in the early 1970s. What was happening here was not a settling of accounts with political enemies, who to a certain extent were prepared for the risks they were taking. This case had nothing whatsoever to do with a struggle between two competing political cliques. It was something far worse: an attack by the totalitarian system on life itself, on the very essence of human freedom and integrity. The objects of this attack were not veterans of old political battles; they had no political past, or even any well-defined political positions. They were simply young people who wanted to live in their own way, to make music they liked, to sing what they wanted to sing, to live in harmony with themselves, and to express themselves in a truthful way. A judicial attack against them, especially one that went unnoticed, could become the precedent for something truly evil: the regime could well start locking up everyone who thought independently and who expressed himself independently, even if he did so only in private. So these arrests were genuinely alarming: they were an attack on the spiritual and intellectual freedom of man, camouflaged as an attack on criminality, and therefore designed to gain support from a disinformed public. Here power had unintentionally revealed its own most proper intention: to make life entirely the same, to surgically remove from it everything that was even slightly different, everything that was highly individual, everything that stood out, that was independent and unclassifiable.

My role, I saw, would be to make use of my various contacts to stir up interest in the affair and to stimulate some action for the support and the defense of these people. I knew that, some time ago, Jiří Němec, a philosopher and psychologist and a former colleague from *Tvář*, had become very close to the underground, and I knew I couldn't do anything without consulting him first. Initially our rapprochement was extremely cautious, mainly on his part, because I had broken with *Tvář* and this still hung between us; as far as the *Tvář* people were concerned, I was practically like Trotsky had been for Stalin. (To be fair, I should add that, when I was in prison after the Charter came out, the *Tvář* people issued a collective position paper in my support.)

Gradually Jiří and I began to get along very well, and we laughed at our old differences (in the meantime, he too had gone through some changes, and was no longer the orthodox *Tvář*-ist he had once been). In the months and years that followed, we became real friends—for the first time, in fact. So Jiří and I began to "direct" the campaign for the Plastics, at least for as long as it was still necessary. The work gave both of us a great deal, and in doing it we were able to give each other something as well. Up to that point, he had deliberately held back from civic, public, or political involvement; he considered his work with the underground, his inconspicuous influence in the Catholic milieu, and his stimulating participation in the independent philosophical movement more important, and he did not want to put all that at risk by coming out in public in a way that would be conspicuous and would certainly lead to conflict. Until that moment, he had been more in favor of working "internally" than "externally." Recognizing that the Plastics could only be helped by a public campaign, he had to change his position, and I think that on this new terrain it was I—since I was more familiar with it, after all—who became his guide. And he, on the other hand, led me out of the confines of "established opposition" and helped me broaden my horizon.

We planned the campaign in detail. Beginning with modest, internal steps, it was intended to build toward more emphatic ones. We wanted to give the regime the opportunity to retreat with dignity. We didn't want to force it to retreat right away behind its own prestige, because then nothing could move it. So, in the initial phase, we went around to different people and tried to get their support. At first we encountered misunderstanding and even resistance, which in that state of affairs was only to be expected. But I have to say that this mistrust evaporated very quickly, far more quickly than we had expected. People in different milieus very quickly began to understand that a threat to the freedom of these young people was a threat to the freedom of us all, and that a strong defense was all the more necessary because everything was against them. They were unknown, and the nature of their nonconformity was a handicap, because even decent citizens might perceive what they were doing as a threat, just as the state had.

The alacrity with which many of those whom we had not expected to have much sympathy for this kind of culture were able to throw off their original inhibitions was clearly related to the situation I've already talked about: this was a time when we were beginning to learn how to walk upright again, a time of "exhaustion with exhaustion," a time when many different groups of people had had enough of their isolation and felt that, if something was going to change, they had to start looking beyond their own horizons. Thus the ground was prepared for some kind of wider, common activity. If the regime's attack on culture had taken place two years earlier, it might have gone by unnoticed.

If I remember correctly, our efforts climaxed with an open letter to Heinrich Böll signed by myself and Jaroslav Seifert,

Václav Černý, and Karel Kosík, and it ultimately resulted in a large petition signed by over seventy people. By that time, the case was known internationally and the media were covering it. (Czechoslovakia had been out of the news for some time, and so the excitement around the Plastics attracted even more attention.) The affair became so generally known that, from then on, the campaign more or less looked after itself. Almost as if we had planned it, which we hadn't, lawyers began to speak up, and finally (which must have been especially shocking for those in high places) even former party functionaries let themselves be heard through the mouth of Zdeněk Mlynář. Thus the spectrum was complete, and though you can't read this directly from the signatures on those protests, it was here, in some connection with the case of the Plastic People—through newly established contacts and friendships—that the main opposition circles, hitherto isolated from each other, came together informally. Later these same groups became the central core of Charter 77.

(At this point, I should perhaps interrupt my reminiscences with another important remark. I'm not giving a history lecture here, I'm merely recalling how I experienced and observed these events at the time. My view may be one-sided; in fact, it probably has to be one-sided. It's a view from the side on which I stood. Others may well have seen differently and might reveal important things that I haven't mentioned. For example, during 1976 certain changes began to be felt among the former communists that had nothing to do with the Plastic People but might have contributed equally to laying the ground for their defense. Collective position papers were published, among them a letter to the Berlin Conference of Communist Parties.)

The state was caught off guard: obviously no one had expected that the case of the Plastic People would arouse so much response. They had assumed it could be settled routinely, as just another criminal case among thousands of others. First they counterattacked with a defamation campaign (a television program against the Plastics and newspaper articles, in *Mladý Svět,* a youth weekly); then they retreated. They began releasing people from custody, and the roster of defendants began to shrink until finally (not counting the smaller trial in Pilzen) they only sent four of them to prison, and their sentences were relatively short, enough to cover the time they had spent in detention or a couple of months longer. The exception was Jirous, who naturally got the longest sentence.

The trial was a glorious event. You may be familiar with the essay I wrote about it. At that time, people interested in the trial could still gather in the corridors of the courthouse or on the stairways, and you could still see the prisoners being brought in in handcuffs and shout greetings to them. Later these possibilities were removed with a speed that corresponded to the speed of the gathering solidarity.

The people who gathered outside the courtroom were a prefiguration of Charter 77. The same atmosphere that dominated then, of equality, solidarity, conviviality, togetherness, and willingness to help each other, an atmosphere evoked by a common cause and a common threat, was also the atmosphere around Charter 77 during its first few months. Jiří Němec and I both felt that something had happened here, something that should not be allowed simply to evaporate and disappear but which ought to be transformed into some kind of action that would have a more permanent impact, one that would bring this something out of the air onto solid ground. Naturally we weren't the only ones who felt this; it was clearly a widespread feeling. We talked to Pavel Kohout about it, and he felt the same way. Zdeněk Mlynář, whom we approached through Vendelín Komeda, was thinking along these lines too.

Our probes ultimately led to the first meeting, which was held on December 10, 1976. It was attended by Mlynář, Kohout, Jiří Němec, me, the owner of the flat where the meeting took place, and Komeda who organized it. There were two subsequent meetings that also included Petr Uhl, Jiří Hájek, and Ludvík Vaculík. Please understand me: Charter 77 belongs to all the Chartists, and it's immaterial which one of them happened to have a hand in preparing the founding document. If I speak of these meetings at all—and this is the first time I've done so—it's only because I know that memory fades and one day perhaps, a careful historian might condemn us for having kept these matters secret so long that we eventually forgot the details. In any case, it was at these meetings that the Charter was prepared. Each one of us discussed the matter in general terms with the people in our own circles, so that even in this embryonic phase quite a few people knew about it. The former communist functionaries around Zdeněk Mlynář had discussed the possibility of establishing some kind of committee to monitor human rights, or a Helsinki Committee along the lines of the one that had been created in the U.S.S.R. But a committee has a necessarily limited number of members who have chosen each other and come to some agreement. The situation here, however, pointed in a different direction, toward the need for a broader and more open association. That was how we came to settle on the notion of a "citizens' initiative."

The point is that it was clear from the beginning—it was the reason for these meetings, not the conclusion they came to—that we should be trying for something more permanent. We were not simply here to write a one-shot manifesto. It was also clear to everyone from the beginning that whatever came out of this would be pluralistic in nature. Everyone would be equal, and no group, regardless of how powerful it might be, would play a leading role or impress its own "handwriting" on the Charter. After the first meeting, the outlines of what we were preparing were still not clear. We only agreed that by the next meeting the proposal for an initial declaration would be drafted. I recall that after this meeting Jiří Němec and I visited Hejdánek, who pointed out that our declaration might be based on the recently issued pacts on human rights. Parallel with that, but also after the first meeting, Mlynář came up with the same idea.

That was how the first draft of the declaration came about. Although I know exactly who wrote it and who added which sentences—or, on the contrary, who struck which sentences out—I don't think it's appropriate to reveal this now, on principle: the original declaration of the Charter is the expression of a collective will. Everyone who signed it stands behind it. And it has become a nice tradition now to emphasize this principle symbolically in, among other things, the silence we maintain about its authorship, though it's clear to everyone that the first signatories could not have written it all at once and together. Perhaps I might say only this, that the name "Charter 77" was Pavel Kohout's idea.

At the next two meetings, the text was edited, every word was carefully considered, we agreed on who would be the first spokesmen, and we also agreed on a method of gathering signatures. It was still not really clear how the Charter would work in practice. As for the spokesmen, it was more or less clear from the outset that Jiří Hájek should be one of them; I understand that, when the ex-communists were thinking about their own committee, Hájek was thought to be the most appropriate chairman. It was Petr Uhl, I believe, who came up with the idea of having three spokesmen. This was generally agreed upon, not only because it would express the pluralistic nature of the Charter, but for various practical reasons as well.

Petr also suggested that I should be another spokesman, although I understand that it was his wife, Anna Šabatová's idea. I had no way of knowing what being spokesman would involve, though I had justifiable fears that it would fully occupy me for God knows how long and leave me no time to write. I didn't really want the job—none of the later spokesmen did either—but I had to accept it. I'd have seemed like a fool if I'd refused to devote myself to a cause I felt so strongly about and invested so much energy and enthusiasm in preparing and had helped persuade others to take up.

I don't know any longer who first suggested Jan Patočka as the third spokesman. Perhaps it was Jiří Němec. I only know that Jiří and I supported his nomination and helped explain why this was an important choice to the others, some of whom were not very familiar with Patočka. It seemed to us that Patočka, who was highly respected in noncommunist cir-cles, not only would be a dignified counterpart to Hájek, but, more than that—and we were almost immediately proved right—we felt that from the outset he, better than anyone else, could impress upon the Charter a moral dimension.

At the time, I paid him several visits, both alone and with Jiří Němec, and I must say that he hesitated for a long time before accepting. He had never before been directly involved in politics, and he'd never had any direct, sharp confronta-tion with the powers that be. In such matters he was reluctant, shy, and reserved. His strategy resembled the strategy of trench warfare: wherever he was, he tried to hold out as long as he could without compromise, but he never went on the attack himself. He was utterly dedicated to philosophy and teaching, and he never modified his opinions, but he did try to avoid things that might have put an end to his work. At the same time, he felt, or so it seemed to me, that one day he would have to put his thinking to the test in action, as it were, that he couldn't avoid it or put it off forever, because ulti-mately this would call his whole philosophy in doubt. He also knew, however, that, if he were to take this final step, he would take it completely, leaving himself no emergency exits, with the same perseverance he devoted to philosophizing. This, of course, might have been another reason for his reluctance. He was certainly not a rash person, and he hesitated a long time before taking any action, but once he had he stood be-hind it to the end.

I think there were others who tried to persuade him to become a spokesman too—I understand his son played an important role in this—but there were some who tried to dissuade him. I myself was involved in one incident, which perhaps was the decisive one: Patočka confided in me that he was also hesitating because of Václav Černý. Černý had been courageously involved in civic affairs all his life, and there were times when he had behaved more directly than Patočka had been able to. He had worked in the underground resistance during the war, and Patočka felt, in short, that Černý had a greater moral right to be a spokesman, and he believed that Černý would feel justifiably left out and resentful of Patočka if the position were not offered to him. It was as though Patočka was simply ashamed to do something he thought was more appropriate for Černý, and he also seemed worried about Černý's possible reaction.

So I went to Černý and laid the cards out on the table. I told him Patočka didn't want to take the job without his blessing, because he thought that Černý was in line ahead of him, but that it was essential to get Patočka for the position precisely because his political profile was not as sharply defined as Černý's and therefore he could function more easily as a binding agent, whereas Černý, who was prickly and outspoken, might well have created a lot of resistance from the outset, and there was no way of guessing how it would affect the work of the Charter. Černý accepted this at once, and I think his acceptance was sincere, without a trace of bitterness. I went back to Patočka and told him about my conversation with Černý, and he was visibly relieved, as though a great weight had fallen from him. So the final hurdle had been overcome: Patočka became a spokesman and plunged into the work, literally sacrificing his life to it. (He died on March 13, 1977, after a prolonged interrogation.) I don't know what the Charter would have become had Patočka not illuminated its beginnings with the clarity of his great personality.

But back to those preparatory meetings. We agreed that the signatures would be gathered slowly, over Christmas, during the normal friendly visits and encounters that take place at that time, so that we wouldn't attract unwanted attention too soon. We named about ten "gatherers," and we roughly outlined for them the circles in which they were to gather signatures. I looked after the technical side of things; I took the text around to the gatherers along with instructions on how it should be signed. I also collected signatures, mainly among my friends, most of whom were writers. We'd already agreed on the day—it was between Christmas and New

Year's—and the hour when all the signatures were to be brought to my place and arranged in an alphabetical list, and everything was to be got ready to be sent to the Federal Assembly, and published. Meanwhile, enough copies of the initial declaration were typed out so that one could be sent to each of the signatories. Everything was supposed to be ready for January 1, 1977, but it was not to be announced until a week later, to allow time to prepare the appropriate publicity, which for various reasons had to be synchronized with the moment when the declaration was to be handed over to the officials.

The day the signatures were to be delivered to my place, I was rather nervous. There were indications that the police already knew something (and it would have been surprising if they hadn't), and I was afraid they would break into my place just when everything had been assembled and we would lose all our signatures. I got even more nervous because, although the meeting was supposed to be at four o'clock, it was almost five and there was still no sign of Zdeněk Mlynář, who was bringing in signatures gathered in ex-communist circles. It turned out there had been a simple misunderstanding about the time, and he eventually arrived, with more than a hundred signatures, which took my breath away. The final tally for the first round was 243 signatures. The police did not show up, we got all the business out of the way, and then a small circle of us drank a toast with champagne.

In that dead period between the completion of our business and the actual explosion, there was one more big meeting at my place, attended by about twenty-five people. We discussed how the Charter would carry on its work and what should be done in what situation and so on. We knew that such a large meeting would probably be impossible to arrange later. Almost everyone was there. It was the first time, for instance, that I had seen Jaroslav Šabata since his recent return from prison. I was asked to run the meeting, and I felt rather strange, giving the floor to former university professors, ministers, and Communist Party secretaries. But it didn't seem strange to anyone else, which is an indication of how strong, even at the beginning, was the feeling of equality within the Charter.

Perhaps I should say something more about plurality within the Charter. It was not easy for everyone—many had to suppress or overcome their ancient inner aversions—but everyone was able to do it, because we all felt that it was in a common cause, and because something had taken shape here that was historically quite new: the embryo of a genuine social tolerance (and not simply an agreement among some to exclude others, as was the case with the National Front government after the Second World War), a phenomenon which—no matter how the Charter turned out—would be impossible to wipe out of the national memory. It would remain in that memory as a challenge that, at any time and in any new situation, could be responded to and drawn on. It was not easy for many noncommunists to make that step, but for many communists it was difficult in the extreme. It was a stepping out toward life, toward a genuine state of thinking about common matters, a transcendence of their own shadow, and the cost of doing so was saying goodbye forever to the principle of the "leading role of the party." Not many former communists actually stood by that slogan anymore, but some of them still carried it in their blood or in their subconscious. It was to the great credit of Zdeněk Mlynář that, with great political subtlety, he recognized the urgency of taking this step, and then used the weight of his authority to persuade those around him to take it.

Was any plan of action worked out at that time?

For a long time, we knew nothing about how the Charter would actually work in practice. Until that larger meeting at my place, the prevailing opinion was that, in addition to various communiqués or position papers on current matters, the Charter should also publish longer and more general thematic documents dealing with various areas of public life. But not even that was very clear beforehand. For example, some of us felt that we should publish only precise documentation regarding particular, individual cases in which human rights had been denied, cases that were, however, somehow typical or significant. In other words, they felt the Charter should function more or less the way the Committee for the Defense of the Unjustly Prosecuted (VONS) did later, the only difference being that the Charter's mandate would not be limited to monitoring violations by the police and the judiciary, but would encompass the whole life of society. At the time, too little was really known. For instance, I was afraid that, despite what it said, many signatories would understand the initial declaration as a one-shot manifesto, and not a commitment to participate in ongoing work. Fortunately, that did not happen.

One of the signature gatherers once said to me there were some signatures you didn't publish. How many people actually signed the Charter?

At this point there are around twelve hundred signatures; I don't know the exact figure, and for various reasons it's pretty difficult to determine. At the beginning there really were about twenty or thirty people who signed the Charter but didn't want their signatures published, at least not right away. We respected this, but later, when the police got their hands on the unpublished signatures as well (they even handed some over for the propaganda writers to use—for example, the signature of Dr. Prokop Drtina), we stopped doing it. Not because it would have been impossible to keep such signatures a secret in future, but because unpublished signatures don't make much sense. If someone sides with the Charter within himself, but for some reason can't sign it publicly, he has dozens of better ways to show this than signing a piece of paper which is then hidden away. So there is no second, underground, super-Charter. Perhaps I should also mention that we tried to dissuade some of our friends from signing the Charter, precisely because their work was so important and so much in the spirit of Charter 77 already that it wasn't worth endangering that work with a signature. This was the case, for example, with Vlasta Třešňák and Jaroslav Hutka, both of whom later signed the Charter anyway.

What happened after the publication of the initial declaration of the Charter is generally well-known and well described, and the history of the Charter, its development, and its social significance have already been written about by historians. I'd rather ask you, therefore, about your first arrest and the period before your third arrest, which is really the beginning of your years in prison.

After the Charter was published and the propaganda campaign against it had started (the state thus effectively gave enormous publicity to the Charter in its very early days), I went through the wildest weeks of my life. At the time, Olga and I were living in Dejvice, a part of Prague which is on the way to Ruzyně Prison, and our flat began to look suspiciously the way the New York Stock Exchange must have looked during the crash of '29, or like some center of revolution. There were interrogations that went on all day long in Ruzyně, but initially everyone was released for the night, and we'd all gather spontaneously at our place to compare notes, draft various texts, meet with foreign correspondents, and make telephone calls to the rest of the world. So ten hours and sometimes longer of being bombarded with questions by investigators was followed by this hectic activity, which wouldn't let up until late at night. Our neighbors were bravely tolerant of all this but, though I had no concrete reason for thinking so, I felt in my bones that the only way this could end for me personally was prison.

My anticipation grew stronger from day to day, until fi-

nally it became a fervent wish that it actually happen, to end
the unnerving uncertainty. On January 14, late in the evening,
after my "normal" interrogation had finished, I was taken
into a large room in Ruzyně where various majors and colo-
nels came in and threatened me with all kinds of terrible
things. They claimed they knew enough about me to get me
at least ten years in prison, that "the fun was over," and that
the working class was "boiling with hatred toward me." Some
time toward morning they shoved me in a cell. Later, when I
was released, I wrote a report about a hundred pages long on
the first days of the Charter, my arrest, and my subsequent
imprisonment; I hid it somewhere, and to this day I have no
idea where it is. Perhaps I'll find it someday.

It's pretty obvious, I think, what the main reason for my
arrest at that time was: I was the youngest of the spokesmen,
I was the only one who had a car, and, quite justifiably, they
thought I was the main motive force behind all the activity,
and the main organizer. Patočka and Hájek were treated as
having a more symbolic significance; they were undoubtedly
more restrained and mild than I was. The authorities obviously hoped that with my arrest the Charter would be crip-
pled.

It was a terrible miscalculation. The Charter may never
have functioned better than during my imprisonment! I know,
from what people have told me, that Patočka and Hájek put
all their strength and all their time into it, and that they personally acted as couriers and organizers. When urged by many
friends to parcel out at least part of his agenda to others,
Patočka apparently replied, "I'm a spokesman and I can still
walk."

To give substance to the official position that the Charter
would be dealt with "politically" and not by locking people
up, the authorities had to formally justify my arrest with
something that had nothing to do with the Charter. That's
why I was tacked onto the case of "Ornest and Co.," which
involved giving texts that had originated inside the country
to the émigré magazine *Svědectví* in Paris. But 90 percent of

the questions during interrogations had to do with the Charter. Moreover, the security officers hoped that by linking my case with that of Ornest they would have material support for the official thesis that the Charter was inspired and directed from abroad. They longed to be able to show that the introductory declaration had been published outside because of my secret connections, via Ornest, with Pavel Tigrid. Of course they didn't manage to prove that—nor could they, because the whole thing was organized in an utterly different way, and far more simply.

For a combination of different reasons, my first period of imprisonment was very hard to bear, but I've already mentioned this in another place in our conversation, and I've written about it as well, and there's no point in repeating myself here. The worst time for me was the final week, when I already suspected that I was about to be released and publicly disgraced at the same time, partly through my own fault. I could only sleep about an hour a day, and I spent the rest of the time in my cell tormenting myself and my cellmate, a petty thief who robbed grocery stores (I wonder where he is now?). He bore it all with great patience, he understood me exactly, and he tried to help me; if I could, I'd buy him a supermarket of his own out of sheer gratitude.

The public disgrace was worse than I'd expected: they said, for instance, that I'd given up the position of spokesman in prison, which wasn't true; the truth is that I had decided to resign (naturally my resignation would have been submitted to those who had entrusted me with the job in the first place, not to the police) for reasons which I still believe were reasonable. But I did not resign while in prison: I merely did the immensely stupid thing of not keeping my intention to resign a secret from my interrogator.

The first days after my return, my state of mind was such that every madhouse in the world would have considered me a suitable case for treatment. In addition to all the familiar, banal symptoms of postprison psychosis, I felt boundless despair mingled with a sort of madcap euphoria. The euphoria was intensified by the discovery that things outside were completely different from the way I'd imagined they would be. The Charter had not been destroyed; on the contrary, it was going through its heroic phase. I was astonished at the scope of its work, at the response it had had, at the explosion of writing it had inspired, at the marvelous atmosphere of solidarity in its midst. I had the intense feeling that, during my few months in prison, history had taken a greater step forward than during the preceding eight years. (Much of the atmosphere of that time has long since evaporated; the heroic period of the Charter has been supplanted by an era of sober and often distressing everyday cares—and if this had not happened, it would have been against all the laws of life and nature.)

In time, of course, I recovered from the psychotic state of those first few days and weeks after my return from prison, but something of the inner contradictions and despair of that time remained within me and marked the two years between my release in May 1977 and my "definitive" imprisonment in May 1979. I became involved in all sorts of ways, and I may have gone somewhat overboard; I was too uptight, if not hysterical, driven by the longing to "rehabilitate myself" from my own public humiliation. I was a cofounder of VONS; I became a spokesman for the Charter again; I engaged in various polemics (about that time, the Charter went through its first crisis, one that was inevitable and completely useful: a new and deeper inquiry into its own meaning). I was even sent to Ruzyně Prison for six more weeks; it was an unsuccessful attempt to put me out of circulation, with the help of a fabricated indictment for disturbing the peace. They were very good weeks indeed. Each week I spent in prison I understood as another small step toward my "rehabilitation," and I took delight in that.

Another factor that contributed to my nervousness, understandably, was the increasing pressure the police put on the Charter and on me personally. I was constantly "shadowed"; there were interrogations; the local authorities plotted against me; I was under house arrest several times, and this was made more piquant by insults and threats; "unknown perpetrators" broke into our dwelling and vandalized it, or they did all sorts of damage to my car. It was an exciting time, what with attacks by the police, escaping from shadows, crawling through the woods, hiding out in the flats of coconspirators, house searches, and dramatic moments when important documents were eaten.

It was also at this time that we had meetings with the Polish dissidents on our common border (the notorious anti-hiker Havel was compelled to walk to the summit of Sněžka five times, but there was a reward: he was able to meet and establish permanent friendships with Adam Michnik, Jacek Kuron, and other members of KOR, the Workers' Defense Committee). I can remember more than one incredible story from that period, the kind of story that to this day I would hesitate to make public, for fear of harming someone. As all of this increased in degree, it became clearer and clearer to me that it would all come to a bad end and that I would most probably end up in prison again.

This time, though, I wasn't afraid of the prospect. I now knew roughly what to expect, I knew that whether my stay in prison was going to have any value in general terms depended entirely on me, and I knew that I would stand the test. I had come to the conclusion—and it may seem overly dramatic to put it like this, but I swear I mean it—that it is better not to live at all than to live without honor. (So there will be no misunderstanding: this is not a standard I apply to others, but the private conclusion of one individual, a conclusion which I have drawn from my own practical experience, and which has proved practical for me in the sense that in extreme situations it simplifies decisions that I have to make about myself.) If my intuition told me that I was headed for prison, as it had in 1977, then this time, unlike 1977, it was not merely a premonition of something unknown, but a clear awareness of what it would mean: quiet perseverance and its unavoidable outcome, several hard years in prison.

When they finally did lock me up during their campaign against VONS, all my former uneasiness suddenly vanished, I was calm and reconciled to what would follow, and I was certain within myself. None of us know in advance how we will behave in an extreme and unfamiliar situation (I don't know, for example, what I would do if I were physically tortured), but if we are certain at least about how we will respond to situations that are more or less familiar, or at least roughly imaginable, our life is wonderfully simplified. The almost four years in prison that followed my arrest in May 1979 constituted a new and separate stage of my life.

In prison, you wrote an extensive book of essays, called Letters to Olga, *but for obvious reasons there is nothing in them about the prison itself. What did you do there? What kind of work were you assigned to?*

When I was in prison, I thought constantly about what I would eventually write about it, and how. I tried to remember all those curious yet moving, comic yet shocking, strange yet typical experiences I had there. I thought about how one day I would describe the incredibly absurd situations I got into. I looked forward at the very least to rendering some colorful, Hrabalesque eyewitness account of the countless, weirdly complex human destinies I encountered there. And I was frustrated by not being able to make even some rudimentary notes on paper.

But when I got out again, I suddenly realized that I would probably never write anything about prison. It's hard to explain why this is; certainly not because my memories of that dark period in my life are too painful or depressing, or because they would open old wounds. I think there is a whole set of different reasons behind it. In the first place, I'm not a narrative author; I can't write stories, and always forget them anyway. In other words, I'm no Hrabal. In the second place, life outside keeps me too busy, and too frequently comes at me with themes of its own, which I experience directly, immediately, right now. It leaves me no time to return to the utterly different and remote world of my years in prison. That world is fading from sight behind a strange haze, and everything in it is blending together in a vague and incommunicable dream. I don't feel a vital need to say anything about it. It seems to belong—as a personal experience—too much to the past, and I'm too preoccupied with the present to be able to go back or produce a sustained evocation of something that was. In the third place, the most important thing about it is incommunicable. No, I mean it: it was a deeply existential and deeply personal experience, and as such I'm simply unable to pass it on. Of course, there are a lot of things that, with a little effort, I could recall and describe, for better or worse, but I'm afraid that, when it comes right down to it, they'd all be superficial things, the surface outlines of events, situations, actions, and characters, not their inner and personally lived essence, and it would probably end up distorting the whole thing rather than doing it justice. You know what I mean: twenty or thirty years ago, in the army, we had a lot of obscure adventures, and years later we tell them at parties, and suddenly we realize that those two very difficult years of our lives have become lumped together into a few episodes that have lodged in our memory in a standardized form, and are always told in a standardized way, in the same words. But in fact that lump of memories has nothing whatsoever to do with our experience of those two years in the army and what it has made of us.

I tried a couple of times, experimentally, to give a coherent account of prison, and each time I realized that, for all my pedantically precise description of all the factographic details, I was missing the essence of things by a fatally wide margin. That remained hidden behind the factography and, in a strange way, was even falsified by it. Enough has been written about prisons and concentration camps, and in that literature are books evoking that experience in a genuinely suggestive and authentic way. I remember, for instance, the marvelous picture of a concentration camp in Peroutka's *The Cloud and the Waltz,* or some passages from Solzhenitsyn or Pecka. But I'm afraid I wouldn't be able to do it—all the more so because I don't feel like doing it. And rather than miss the meaning of that experience, it's better not to deal with it at all. So I'd rather not talk about prison at all, though I will respond to the concrete part of your question.

In Heřmanice I first worked on a spot welder, and I welded together metal gratings. For several months I couldn't fill the quota, but fellows twenty years younger, physically stronger, and accustomed to physical work couldn't fill it either. In any case, that's why they assigned me to that work, so that when I failed to fulfill the quotas they'd have an excuse to go on tormenting me in all sorts of different ways. The so-called nonfulfillers in prison are pariahs among pariahs; they're punished in various ways, used for work after work, and given less food (that didn't bother me), and their pocket money is docked, and they are constantly accused of loafing and ridiculed for it by the police and some of the other prisoners. After several months I was assigned to better work (the contrast between my work classification and my fitness was starting to be noticeable, and there was a danger that news of my health would get out), but I must add that it was at a time when I was beginning to fulfill the norms after all, which gave them fewer opportunities to torment and exploit me.

Next I worked with a big oxyacetylene welder, cutting flanges out of enormous, thick pieces of metal. Jiří Dienstbier and I took turns on it, and both of us fulfilled the quotas. After I was shifted to Bory, I worked in the laundry, which was a very exclusive place to work (the human relationships were worse there, however: almost everyone informed on everyone else), and finally I was assigned to work in a scrap-metal plant, where I stripped the insulation off wires and cables; even that wasn't too bad, as long as you could get used to the cold and the endless filth. Work in prisons is slave labor but it's also intended to be punishment. The quotas are double what they would be in civilian life. To that I should add that in prison of the first correctional category, where I was, work is generally considered by the prisoners as a psychological rest, and they all look forward to it: the remainder of the day provides better opportunities for general harassment, which is the main instrument of "rehabilitation."

Tell me something about your letters from prison. Where and when did you get the idea to conceive of them as a book?

I'd much rather talk about that, and, moreover, it seems to me that I owe a certain explanation to readers of the book. So, when fate swept Benda, Dienstbier, and me from detention in Ruzyně to the camp in Heřmanice (to our astonishment, it swept us all there together), we found ourselves in a territory ruled by an absolutist and much-feared, half-demented warden (he was feared not only by the prisoners but by the guards as well), for whom we became a sort of plum at the end of his prison career. In the 1950s, as a boy of scarcely more than twenty, he was put in charge of a labor camp where fifteen hundred of the two thousand prisoners under him were politicals—professors, ministers, and bishops (so he boasted to me at least once). Now, for many long years, as a man of high rank and great merit, covered with medals, he could exercise his limitless powers only on pickpockets, rapists, and, at the very best, some fallen deputy ministers (usually in for embezzlement). And so, with our arrival, he found a belated self-justification: once again he had political prisoners in his jurisdiction, with the added bonus that we were from the "central *nomenklatura*" of dissent—that is, our names were generally well known from foreign broadcasts, from our former work, and from witch-hunts in *Rudé Pravo*. And so he really had a time with us.

He was a genuinely dangerous person, and quite unpredictable. One memory in particular may reveal something of his character: once, in our presence, he sighed and said in genuine envy, "Hitler did things differently—he gassed vermin like you right away!" (Once he shouted at me how much he'd love to put me up against the wall and shoot me; one of the things that obviously bothered him about Husák was that, as a former political prisoner, Husák deprived him of such opportunities; I, on the contrary—I must confess—found my-self thinking well of Husák at that moment.) He had his sights fixed on me in particular because he expected me to be the "weak link" in our threesome. My awkward politeness obvi-ously created that impression (Dienstbier writes about this in his afterword to the Czech edition of my prison letters). I mention this now because one area where this man could really find some kind of self-fulfillment, politically and per-sonally, was our letters home. We were strictly forbidden to write anything of any kind, but he couldn't very well forbid us to write letters, because we had a legal right to do so.

We were allowed to write one four-page letter home a week. It had to be legible, with nothing corrected or crossed out, and there were strict rules about margins and graphic and stylistic devices (we were forbidden, for example, to use quotation marks, to underline words, use foreign expressions, etc.). Our letters gave him endless opportunities to harass us, punish us, insult us, and humiliate us. He would strictly for-bid us to write about anything except "family matters." Hu-mor was banned as well: punishment is a serious business, after all, and jokes would have undermined the gravity, which is one of the reasons why my letters are so deadly serious, without a trace of humor or irony. If we wanted our letters to get through, we had to observe these foolish injunctions, but thanks to this we gradually got used to all those limita-tions and completely adapted to them. In my letters—even those I wrote later from Bory—you won't find a single un-derlined word, for example.

Despite this strict censorship and the risk that we might cause more difficulties, and despite the desperate lack of space, time, and opportunity to concentrate on writing, all three of us slowly began to find, in our letters home, our own self-fulfillment, obviously a complex sort of self-fulfillment compared with the censorial self-fulfillment of the warden. Slowly, with great difficulty and many failures, we began to smuggle into our letters various meditations, or at least we tried. The obstacles merely intensified the need: besides all the other things the letter writing meant to us, it became a kind of sport as well. Will we get something past the warden this time or won't we? Will we be able to write something meaningful or won't we? It became a passion. And for me— I can't speak for the others—it became something that gave my stay in prison a meaning.

By the very nature of things in prison, you're forced to think a little more about yourself, about the meaning of your actions, about questions pertaining to your own Being. The letters gave me a chance to develop a new way of looking at myself and examining my attitudes to the fundamental things in life. I became more and more wrapped up in them: I came to depend on them to the point where almost nothing else mattered. All week long I would develop my essays in my head—at work, during exercises, before going to bed—and then on Saturday, amid constant interruption, I would write them out in a kind of wild trance. At first, for reasons of time, it was impossible for me to write a rough draft first. Later I discovered ways of doing it, but once I'd written out a fair copy, I wasn't allowed to change anything or cross anything out, much less copy it over. I'd hand it in; then there'd be a short, suspenseful wait: would it get through or not? Since I wasn't allowed to keep a copy, I eventually lost track of what I had written, when I'd written it and how, and which letters had been sent or held back, which is why there are so many gaps, repetitions, and flaws in logic.

In time, of course, I learned how to think ahead and ar-range my thoughts in thematic cycles, and to weave the motifs in and out of them, and thus—somewhat intermittently—to build, over time, my own little structure, putting it together somewhat like my plays. I invented concepts and categories, experimented with them, tried them out in different contexts, and then, after a while, either dropped them or came back to them again and again, in an obsessive attempt to touch, as precisely as possible, my feeling or experience. The letters, in fact, are endless spirals in which I've tried to enclose something. Very early on, I realized that comprehensible letters wouldn't get through, and that only a letter as complicated and thorny as possible would stand a fighting chance. That too became unconscious habit after a while, which is why there are all those long compound sentences and complicated ways of saying things. Instead of writing "regime," for instance, I would obviously have had to write "the socially apparent focus of the non-I," or some such nonsense.

It was clear to us from the beginning that our letters were circulating among our friends, and that it was proper that this should happen, and so we got used to the fact that our contact with our families was a public matter and that our letters, written rapidly to the accompaniment of the shouting of our fellow prisoners, were treated as literary artifacts, as reports to the world about the state of our souls. From there, it was only a short step to thinking of them as a book. Again, I have to emphasize how distressing the external conditions were. For example, when I managed to write out the rough draft of a letter, the problem of where to hide it arose. I wasn't allowed to have drafts, and searches were a daily routine. In Bory, for instance, I worked in the laundry, on a machine called a *kalandra,* which is something between a wringer and an iron; I hid my rough drafts in a mountain of dirty sheets stained by millions of unborn children, and I would revise them during the noon break, while trying to avoid being seen by informers (and mainly by a certain O.J., a monstrous figure), for whom they would have provided a marvelous opportunity for ratting on me.

Naturally I assumed that if the letters were ever read, or published in samizdat or outside the country, only the ambitious philosophical passages would be published, and not the matter-of-fact passages meant for Olga (the ones separated from the abstract passages by an asterisk), in which, in my own pedantic way, I made unrealistic requests, ordered what

I wanted her to send, and so on. I asked my old friend from *Tvář* Jan Lopatka to prepare my letters from prison for publication, and it is to his great credit that he ignored my directions and kept a balanced proportion of those private matters as well. Thanks to his idea, it's clear that the book is a book of letters from prison, not essays written in the peace and quiet of my study. The existential background of those meditations is uncovered and made present, and it may well give the book life and drama, if it can have such qualities at all.

The result is a very strange book, and to this day I'm not sure exactly what it is. Is it a collection of essays? A document? A document of what, exactly? Of me? Of prison? Once upon a time, writing those letters helped to save my life and give it a meaning, but what can they mean to others, outside the prison world? Does anyone, amid the rush of contemporary life, in the age of digests and digests, have the time to hack their way through those tangled, thorny sentences and search out a meaning in them? The letters contain nothing about prison, and one could scarcely learn anything about prison from them. And as philosophy? The world—in the West, at least—is flooded with thousands of far more readable and probably more penetrating books written by real philosophers who didn't have to write quickly, surrounded by noise, and had all the books in the world to quote from. Given that, what is one to make of a strange book like *Letters to Olga*? I have to admit that I admire anyone who has read it all and understood it; there are many passages that I simply don't understand myself anymore. And whenever I meet someone who has actually got something out of the book, who has recognized, in my own clumsy search for myself in prison, something of his own search, and who has read it not only with understanding but with a certain excitement as well, I am always deeply moved, perhaps more so than my most enthusiastic reader, and that person has all my admiration and thanks.

You live in Germany, and so you know that the book market in Germany is awash with tens of thousands of books of every kind, and that, in this era of television and video, people read very little. How do you explain the fact that the German translation of my queer book was bought by over four thousand people? I don't understand it, but of course I'm glad: it's another four thousand little stones to shore up my conviction that the Lord didn't send me to prison in vain.

Do you think you fulfilled the goals you set for yourself after you were sentenced? Did you come back from prison a more balanced person? Did you reconstitute yourself psychically and mentally, as you'd planned in letter 14?

Once I was sentenced, I knew for certain that I'd be spending several years in prison. That kind of assurance, regardless of how well one is prepared for it, is an important watershed. Suddenly the hierarchy of one's values is changed. One's chronological perspective is altered, and everything takes on a different meaning. I'm an inveterate bureaucrat, and finding my bearings in this new situation meant above all making a plan. It was a kind of instantaneous auto-therapy.

I also knew that I would be better able to bear prison if I could manage to breathe some positive significance into it, turn it around to work in my favor, give it a value. I've already mentioned the despair I felt during the two years before my arrest, and the uptightness and excessive behavior that resulted. It was easy enough, therefore, to see that I would have to use that endless period when—as I imagined then—I would be no more than a tiny, anonymous screw in the enormous prison machinery, to find inner calm, to rediscover the balance I once had, and to gain some kind of perspective on things. I remembered, rather nostalgically, how I'd been in the sixties, a balanced, cheerful fellow with a healthy, ironic distance from everything, and not constantly bogged down in trauma and depression. Of course, I was no doubt idealizing my own youth, and my notions of what it would be like to serve my sentences were immensely naïve. I had even hoped to write plays in prison, learn new languages, and God knows what else!

An even greater illusion was my hope that I would have peace and quiet in prison, and that I would be no more than "a tiny, anonymous screw"! Just the opposite happened. Prison was an endless chain of nerve-racking situations; I found myself being observed and monitored by an infinitely greater number of watchful eyes than during my darkest time in freedom. In a few days, I understood how foolish, at least externally, my plans had been. But this doesn't mean that I gave them up entirely. So I tried, along another, immensely more tortuous little path, to proceed in that general direction, or at least to act in the spirit of my original plans. And as I've already said, my letters were immensely helpful in that regard. They were the only thing left that I could really do, and they became an area in which I tried to do something with myself, to achieve something, to clarify something.

I'm not the best judge of whether I returned from prison a more balanced man or not. I may have rid myself of that excessiveness I felt before my arrest. Yet some things are worse than before. I'm less capable of spontaneous delight, my periods of spleen are more frequent, and I need even more dogged determination to carry out the tasks I set for myself. My wife says I hardened in prison. I don't know. If I have worsened, then it has only touched my inner self, my intimate self, my private self. In my work I may well be genuinely more balanced, more tranquil, and perhaps more understanding and tolerant too, and perhaps I've achieved a greater perspective. If I look over what I've done since my release, from the plays and essays I've written right down to less obvious civic acts, I have the impression that these things are true. (After all, even *Largo Desolato,* which is obviously my most personal play, is essentially a rather cold and surgical work!) Whether my impression is correct, however, is something best left to others to decide; I am truly not the most competent judge in these matters! But this progress—if it really is progress—is not free: it is obviously being paid for by a decline in my ability to be quite simply happy as a physical being.

While you were still in custody, before your trial, you were offered the chance to emigrate, and although you rejected the offer in no uncertain terms, you often mention, in your letters from prison, that you dreamed of Miloš Forman. Forman is now a successful film director in the U.S.A. Is there some kind of unconscious or subconscious connection there?

Possibly. Forman is an old friend of mine, and his success, contrasted with my miserable position as a prisoner, may have influenced those dreams. But I don't think they were the main influence. There were other things that may have been more important. But this is mere conjecture; I'm not Freud or Jung, and I don't know how to interpret dreams, and, in any case, I'm afraid it's impossible to get to the bottom of their mystery. I have never regretted refusing the chance to travel to the U.S.A. (it was never presented as a chance to emigrate) and my choice to remain in prison instead.

Anyone reading your Letters to Olga *and comparing them, for instance, with Čapek's letters to his Olga, would be surprised not to find a single lyrical letter—that is, a real, personal letter to Olga. Wasn't she annoyed with you for that? Would you be willing to say something about her, about your relationship with her, and about what she means to you?*

As is often the case with mortals, I too have had various emotional relationships in my life, and I certainly have more than one sin on my heavenly tally-sheet. Even so, there is one certainty in my life that nothing—so far, at least—has been able to shake. That certainty is Olga. We've known each other for thirty-three years, we've been together for thirty, and for those thirty years we've gone through everything possible and impossible together. That, if nothing else, binds us together, and will probably continue to do so.

Olga and I are very different. I'm a child of the middle class, always the diffident intellectual. Olga's a working-class girl, very much her own person, sober, unsentimental, and she can even be somewhat mouthy and obnoxious; in other words, as we say, you can't get her drunk on a bun. I grew up in the loving and firm embrace of a dominant mother, and I needed an energetic woman beside me to turn to for advice and yet still be someone I could be in awe of. In Olga, I found exactly what I needed: someone who could respond to my own mental instability, offer sober criticism of my wilder ideas, provide private support for my public adventures. All my life, I've consulted with her in everything I do (the wags claim I even require her approval of the sins by which I hurt her, and that I seek her advice in the problems my occasional emotional centrifugality bring me). She's usually first to read whatever I write, and if not, then she's certainly my main authority when it comes to judging it.

Her ability to express feelings that my chronic politeness would never allow me to express has occasionally protected me from the turmoil of the world and the danger that I might become lost in it entirely. I can imagine a more ideal lifetime partner, but, oddly enough, I can't imagine living with anyone else (which has brought unhappiness to more than one rare creature, which I then bear with as much difficulty as she).

Olga and I have not professed love for each other for at least two hundred years, but we both feel that we are probably inseparable. But there's another factor here. In prison, you are like a child in that everything is decided for you by some-one else. Prison robs a person of his independence, and the helplessness and defenselessness of the prisoner intensifies his dependence on the absent spouse. She is the only member of his real world with whom he can correspond; he can see her occasionally, for a brief visit, and therefore she becomes the central representative of that real world; she is its ruler and its still center, and ultimately she becomes the only focus of all his hope, and the only assurance that life has a meaning. (Prisoners' wives generally don't see the onus this places on them; they tend to divorce or abandon their men en masse, heedless of the fact that prisoners find it far harder to cope with marriage breakups than fellows on the outside.)

It's true that you won't find many heartfelt, personal passages specifically addressed to my wife in my prison letters. Even so, I think that Olga is their main hero, though admittedly she's a hidden hero. That was why I put her name in the title of the book. Doesn't that endless search for a firm point, for certainty, for an absolute horizon that fills those letters say something, in itself, to confirm that?

Occasionally my abstract meditations annoyed Olga. She is very matter-of-fact in all things, and it's not surprising that she longed for a "personal note." I remember that Kamila Bendová once wrote to Vašek Benda, when he was in Heřmanice with me, that in my letters—unlike his—there was not a single kind word. Vašek gave me her letter to read, and I tried to write a love letter to Olga. The result was a strange study which Vašek said contained only one heartfelt emotion: anger at Kamila for forcing me into writing it. Olga and I have really never made a habit of professing our feelings for each other. We're both reticent, though this reticence has a different source in each of us: pride in her case, shame in mine. But I've said enough. I don't want my wife—when she reads this—to be too pleased with herself, nor would I want Vašek Benda to say that the only sign of warmth in my answer was anger at you for asking me that question.

I don't think he'd say that. Your prison era came to an end with your early release for health reasons in 1983. Is it true that your life was in danger?

In the fall of 1982, there were several indications that led me to believe the prison authorities would be glad to be rid of me. Obviously they realized that I was a bigger political liability as a prisoner than I would be as a free man. Prison had not derailed me, and I had shown that I could stick it out—in other words, it hadn't worked as punishment. And international interest in my case was growing rather than slacking off. While I was wringing out those thousands of sperm-stained sheets each day and composing Heideggerean mediations in my head, universities abroad conferred honorary degrees on me, and statesmen would bring my name up when they had talks with our representatives, which was no doubt something our politicians could have done without. A big peace congress was scheduled to take place the following spring in Prague, and they wanted to get some big-name writers to come to it (as far as I know, none did anyway), and they would not have been pleased had my famous colleagues spoken about me there in public.

The first sign that they were inclining toward sending me home was an unexpected visit from my Prague investigators. Their message was that, if I would write them a single sentence asking for pardon, I would be home in a week. It was clear to me why: in a week, Dr. Husák was to go on a state visit to Austria, and he wanted to present my release as a gift to the Austrian president (he had been ambassador to Prague, and we had met—he was the one who announced to me, for example, that I'd been awarded an Austrian state prize for European literature). Dr. Husák, however, does not like backing down, and if he must, he tries to implicate his opponent as well, which is why he didn't just grant me the pardon directly, but required me to make this little gesture in the form of a request.

It went against the grain, but I wasn't entirely sure. If this offer was the result of some intervention from abroad, those who had intervened would see it as absurd stubbornness on my part if I were to refuse to write a single sentence (elsewhere, a request for pardon does not carry with it the tinge of humiliation it does here), and next time they might not bother to intervene on anyone's behalf. I set a curious condi-

tion: I demanded the right to consult three of my fellow prisoners. I was allowed to meet with them for seven (I don't
know why seven, exactly) minutes, in the presence of a guard,
of course. The decision was that I shouldn't ask for pardon.
So I refused, and the Austrian president probably got a cut-
glass vase instead.

But that wasn't the only indication. There were health reasons, which I assume were also taken into consideration. And
they were far worse than any of us could have expected. One
Sunday afternoon in late January 1983, I suddenly came down
with a high fever; my whole body began to ache, I was shak-
ing, incapable of talking or moving about, and I had no idea
what was happening to me. At night, I trembled so violently
that the whole bunk shook and my fellow prisoners couldn't
sleep. My heart was beating wildly, and I thought I might be
dying. I'd never been on the point of death before, and of
course I didn't know how you recognized it, but my state was
so terrifying that I couldn't help wondering. By morning, my
temperature had gone down and I reported for sick call, fearing all the while that I wouldn't have a temperature and would
be punished for malingering, which was common in Bory. It
turned out well: I had a temperature of almost 104 degrees
Fahrenheit. I wondered what it had been during the night.

They took me to the clinic, where I lay in bed for several
days. My condition showed no improvement (I ate scarcely
anything for a week, and must have looked terrible). They fed
me aspirin but otherwise paid no special attention to me; they
probably thought it was a normal bout of flu. After about
three days, with the help of a male nurse I knew, I managed
to persuade them to examine me. They X-rayed my lungs and
administered antibiotics at once, but they wouldn't tell me
what the matter was. I suspected it was pneumonia again (I
had had it several times already in prison). But from the
heightened interest in my case I got the feeling it was more
complicated than that.

Then one day, with my temperature still around 104, they
suddenly led me away in my pajamas, handcuffed me, stuck

me into an ambulance, and drove off. It was a ghastly journey; I was buffeted about, my lungs and my whole body ached, because my hands were bound I couldn't catch hold of anything, and I could scarcely breathe. But a kind of prisoner's pride would not let me ask them to take the cuffs off. We arrived at Pankrác Prison in Prague (a journey of about ninety miles from Pilzen), they put me in the prison hospital, and I was in isolation—that is, alone in my cell, which was good.

And there they gave me a thorough examination and started treatment. On top of it, I think I may have had pleurisy and some other related complications; at first there was talk of a kind of bubble in my lungs. My temperature went down, and I began to eat a bit. I wrote about everything to Olga, including my uncertainty, during those first two days, about whether I would live or die. I knew that the censorship at Pankrác was milder, so I risked it. The letter got through. Immediately Olga and Zdeněk Urbánek went to Pankrác and demanded to see me. This was impossible, of course. They asked if they could leave me some fruit. That was impossible too. Olga asked for details. They told her I was all right. So she got angry, went home, and called Pavel Kohout in Vienna. Pavel was wonderful. He's always been able to react quickly and practically and correctly in crises, and that's exactly what he did this time: he called everyone he could think of, including various chancellors of Western European states. Interventions in my behalf began arriving, and the fight to save my life began, though of course it had already been saved in Pankrác (if it had ever been seriously in danger, that is). While this was going on, they evidently came to the conclusion somewhere that the state of my health offered them a reason to release me.

One evening, which I shall never forget, just as I was getting ready to go to sleep, into my cell there suddenly stepped several guards, a doctor, and a woman official of some kind, who informed me that Prague District Court 4 was terminating my sentence. I was flabbergasted and asked them if I could spend one more night in prison. They said it was out of the question, because I was now a civilian. I asked them what I was supposed to do now, in my pajamas. An ambulance was waiting to take me to a civilian hospital, they said. It was a shock to hear the doctor suddenly calling me "Mr. Havel" instead of just "Havel." I hadn't heard myself addressed that way in years.

I got into the ambulance, and I couldn't understand why they didn't handcuff me, why there was no policeman with a dog along, why I wasn't even locked in. My main thought was that I could jump out anytime I felt like it! They took me to the Pod Petřínem Hospital and put me in the intensive-care unit. I called home at once, and Olga, Ivan, and his wife came and brought me some things. Shortly after that, the news of my release was broadcast on the Voice of America. Only the day before, they had broadcast a Charter 77 appeal for my release. There must have been hell to pay for the censor who allowed my letter out of Pankrác. It was thanks to his laxness that the campaign to save me had been launched, and what was originally intended to appear as an unexpected and generous gesture on the part of the regime suddenly seemed like abject capitulation to the campaign, and an admission that they didn't know how to handle my illness and were afraid that I might die on their hands.

That month in the hospital was probably the most beautiful month of my life. Released from the burden of prison, but not yet encumbered by the burden of freedom, I lived like a king. All day long, friends came to visit me (once I counted fifteen of them in the room at one time) and they brought me gifts, mainly samizdat texts. Olga brought me a bottle of gin a day, and I was able to convert all those fruit compotes people were constantly bringing me for my health into a fruit punch, which I would drink at night with the young nurses (just imagine—you scarcely see a woman for four years, and suddenly they plop you down among ten fresh nursing-school grads!). When I wasn't drinking with them, I spent the whole night reading *The Czech Dream Book* by Ludvík Vaculík, the pivotal work of that time, which everyone said I had to read first. Flowers poured in from all over the world.

The hospital was kind to me; I had various perks—visiting hours, for example, did not apply to me. There was a silent agreement between the State Security forces, the hospital administration, and me that they would let me do whatever I wanted in return for not receiving foreign journalists or making telephone calls abroad while in the hospital. The world—beginning with loved ones and friends and ending with the doctors, nurses, and fellow patients—showed me its kindest face. I had no responsibilities, only rights. I was no longer in prison and, at the same time, I did not yet know the post-prison depression suffered by a returnee who is suddenly cast loose into the absurd terrain of freedom. Even the investigators who came to see me were like honey and very delicately suggested that I oughtn't to spread stories about the circumstances of my illness and the medical treatment I had received in prison. I had to laugh: it was the last thing in the world that interested me then!

But the beautiful dream had to end. The day came when I had to step back into the world as it really was. This was at the beginning of March, just a little more than three years ago, and I've been moving along its uncertain surface ever since. A new stage in my life had begun, and I'd rather not talk about that until later, when I have more distance from it, when I know better what to think about it.

V

The Politics of Hope

In your essay "Politics and Conscience" from 1984, you refer to the Czech philosopher Václav Bělohradský, who teaches at the university in Genoa, Italy. Bělohradský was a student of Patočka. What attracts you to his work? Is there any connection between your idea of "self-momentum" and Bělohradský's "eschatology of the impersonal"?

After returning from prison, I came across, more or less by accident, Bělohradský's book *The Crisis of the Eschatology of the Impersonal.* I was extraordinarily taken with it. Many things which I had felt myself in a similar way, Bělohradský expressed beautifully and persuasively, and moreover he connected it all into a consistent whole, which clarified for me many relationships I had been unaware of. I like the book for its language too. Bělohradský's writing is rich in compression, metaphor, and unusual associations. Occasionally it is more poetic than philosophical, in the traditional sense, and therefore Bělohradský cannot always be taken at his word and literally.

After reading this book, I began looking for more of his work, which was scattered about in various exile journals. Then I gathered them together, along with several essays by other authors, whose work derived from his or who examined his themes, and I made an anthology of them. It's called *The Natural World as a Political Problem,* and it was published in my own Edice Expedice. Meanwhile, I began to correspond with Bělohradský, and I even wrote an afterword for the anthology. The essay of mine you refer to, "Politics and Conscience," was considerably influenced by Bělohradský's point of view.

By the "self-momentum" of a power or a system I mean the blind, unconscious, irresponsible, uncontrollable, and unchecked momentum that is no longer the work of people, but which drags people along with it and therefore manipulates them. It's obvious that this self-momentum is in fact the momentum of the impersonal power that Bělohradský talks about. He sees signs of the twilight or crisis of the eschatology of this power in the same things I find them in. I should add, however, that, unlike me, Bělohradský is a philosopher, and his explications are widely and solidly grounded, whereas I am only an occasional essayist or a philosophically inclined literary man, and it would be inappropriate to treat us as two commensurate quantities, or even as belonging to the same family.

In an interview I did with Bělohradský not long ago, which was also published in your Edice Expedice as Thinking Green, *Bělohradský says, "I am one of the vanquished. As a Czech, as an exile, as a European, as an intellectual, as a philosopher, and as an Italian citizen ... this is how I see the role of the vanquished intellectual: we must not let ourselves be corralled into histories written by the victors." Do you identify with this concept of the role of the intellectual?*

If Bělohradský sees the most intrinsic role of the intellectual in not allowing himself to be corralled into histories written by the victors, then I fully agree. He seems to be saying, in different words, what the French philosopher André Glucksmann has said. Glucksmann was recently in Prague, and I had a long conversation with him that went far into the night. Glucksmann says the role of the intellectual is to warn, to predict horrors, to be a Cassandra who tells us what is going on outside the walls of the city. I share this notion, whether in Glucksmann's version or Bělohradský's. I too think the intellectual should constantly disturb, should bear witness to the misery of the world, should be provocative by being independent, should rebel against all hidden and open pressure and manipulations, should be the chief doubter of systems, of power and its incantations, should be a witness to their mendacity. For this very reason, an intellectual cannot fit into any role that might be assigned to him, nor can he ever be made to fit into any of the histories written by the victors. An intellectual essentially doesn't belong anywhere; he stands out as an irritant wherever he is; he does not fit into any pigeonhole completely. This is obviously true of Bělohradský himself. The Czech exiles have a continuing problem with where to put him.

An intellectual is always at odds with hard and fast categories, because these tend to be instruments used by the victors. To this extent I agree with Bělohradský. The notion of the vanquished, however, is more complicated. Yes, to a certain extent an intellectual is always condemned to defeat. He's like Sisyphus in that regard. And there's always something suspect about an intellectual on the winning side. And yet in another, more profound sense the intellectual remains, despite all his defeats, undefeated—again like Sisyphus. He is in fact victorious through his defeats. His position, therefore, is ambiguous. Not to admit that such an ambiguity exists could ultimately mean accepting a place in history as written by the victors. For do not the victors assign to Bělohradský, and perhaps even more to me, the role of the defeated? And if we confirm this status, aren't we confirming their histories as well? Of course, in a certain sense I am defeated, but in another sense I do not feel defeated at all. Sometimes—paradoxically—I find myself slightly horrified at how bound I am by my undefeatedness and therefore by the extent to which I do not fit into the victors' histories.

Here in the West, I sometimes see the Czechs or the Poles accused of provincialism; at other times I've seen you touted

*as one of the most important fighters for peace, but I don't
think I've ever read of anyone's accepting your basic idea
about the threat to human identity and then going on to ask
whether this identity is also threated in West Germany, in
Sweden, or in England. The mass media here never seem to
admit the possibility that the problem you raise might be a
general problem. Doesn't that bother you sometimes?*

I'm not an important enough intellectual authority that
everyone should have to deal with my ideas. But I know that
people in the West in general tend not to admit that humanity is in a state of crisis and that therefore their own humanity
is in a state of crisis too. Whenever I have a chance to talk to
Westerners, I try to raise this matter.

Here's a small recent example of this Western shortsight-
edness: For years now, the entire West has known that Kha-
daffi is a terrorist, and for years the West has bought oil from
him and helped him extract it from the ground. So, in fact,
the West has cultivated him and continues to support him.
To this day, they haven't been able to put together a decent
embargo against him. In other words, Westerners are risking
their security and their basic moral principles for the sake of
a few barrels of crude oil. Particular interests take precedence
over general interests. Everyone hopes the bomb will not fall
on him. And then, when the situation becomes untenable, the
only thing anyone can think of doing is bombing Libya. It is
a truncated and primitive reaction.

*In the West there has been a gradual change in the inter-
pretation of the laws regarding political asylum. Asylum is
more and more clearly being seen as an escape from tyranny,
but not as an escape from totalitarian systems. The disintegration of meaning or the existence of a coercive atheistic
and collective educational system is no longer considered
sufficient reason for granting political asylum. How would
you explain to Western governments that the totalitarian*

state represents just as serious a danger for the individual as
a tyranny?

Western governments don't ask me what I think, but I
always try to throw some light on the subject wherever I can.
I frequently find people intellectually or theoretically agree-
ing with my opinions, but I seldom encounter genuine understanding. But I'm not surprised: some experiences are
simply untransferable and can't be explained; they can only
be understood when one undergoes them oneself. On the
other hand, of course, I must say that, as far as the rights of
asylum go, I am not sure that it's appropriate simply to condemn Western governments. Totalitarian or authoritarian regimes exist in most parts of the world. And I doubt whether
all their inhabitants who find the regimes unsuitable would
fit into a few democratic countries. Western governments,
therefore, are unfortunately forced to choose, and on the
whole it's logical of them to give priority to those whose lives
are immediately threatened by a tyranny, over those who simply do not like—as you say—how their children are being
educated.

But I would go even further: I don't think it hurts occasionally to remind people who live in totalitarian states, subtly perhaps, that they might also do something about their
own domestic totalitarianism, instead of just running away
from it. If I demand that Westerners not think merely of their
own particular interests and that they behave as all of us
should behave—that is, as though we were immediately responsible for the fate of the whole of society—then I see no
reason why I shouldn't demand the same of people living in
totalitarian countries. This may sound harsh, and in fact I
don't think in such harsh terms myself, but unfortunately,
when I heard your question, I began to see in my mind's eye
all those familiar people whose spines are bent, who are cautious, who inconspicuously support and create totalitarianism
and then, on their very first trip abroad, suddenly decide that
they'd rather live in a country where the living is easier, and

they immediately demand the rights and glory due to political refugees. Why is it that over there in the West they see all these rights as a natural responsibility of government, whereas when they were here they contributed in all sorts of ways to a state in which individuals have no rights at all? I would never dare to ask anyone to shed his blood for our freedom, but I have no hesitation in suggesting that it might make more sense to criticize the atheistic educational system here, rather than running away to the God in the West.

Do you follow Czech exile literature? What do you think about it? Is there anything that has pleasantly surprised you or, shall we say, turned you off?

Even though I have better access to Czech exile literature than most of my countrymen, I have to admit that I don't know it very well and I don't follow it systematically. In recent years I've had two great experiences. The first was a wonderful novel by Ferdinand Peroutka called *The Cloud and the Waltz,* one of the best Czech novels I know of in the last few decades. And I am very fond of Škvorecký's *The Engineer of Human Souls.*

But I'd like to return to the second half of the question: Is there anything about exile literature you don't like? Is there something coming out of exile you don't think belongs, something that may even irritate you?

Yes, there is—some of the things that appear in some exile magazines. I've occasionally read silly things from the pen of those relentless anticommunist war-horses. For example, I read that all of us back home are left-wing (green Bolsheviks), and even that we're all agents of Moscow in disguise. I don't know whether I'm left-wing or right-wing, but I have to admit

that, when I'm confronted with this type of right-wing spiri-
tuality, I inevitably find myself leaning to the left.

*In Prague one sometimes hears harsh criticism of Milan
Kundera, which is perhaps a reaction to his worldwide literary success—perhaps the first time this has happened to a
Czech author. (For example, his last book,* The Unbearable
Lightness of Being, *sold more than two hundred thousand
copies in Italy and became the top-selling foreign book ever in
postwar Italy. The book has had similar success in the
U.S.A., and of course in France.) Doesn't this raise the question of why there is such a split between domestic literary
taste and the taste of the rest of Europe?*

I don't quite understand why a difference of opinion over
one book or one author ought to mean that there is a fundamental split with the rest of Europe. Nor do I understand
why such a "split" should automatically be blamed on the one
who does the splitting. But whatever the case may be, I think
it's better to have one's own opinion, even if that means a
split, than to try to avoid a split by giving up one's own point
of view. I personally like Kundera's book, and that has nothing to do with how many copies were sold. And, anyway, isn't
this continuing fear of being out of step with the rest of the
world a clear sign of provincialism? To the extent that I know
Kundera's literary loves, it seems to me that he—unlike some
of his apologists in exile—does not suffer from this type of
provincialism.

*What do you think about the problem of a national literature
trying to be "world-class"?*

Nothing. At most I think it's a traditional Czech pseudo-
problem.

*I admit that "world-class" is an overworked and misleading
term these days, but I think it was Goethe who first introduced the idea of a kind of golden literary treasury on which
mankind, regardless of his nationality, could continue to draw
to understand himself and his history. Now, in some countries, Milan Kundera is already treated as such a classic. If
you'll allow me, I'd like to quote something from an article
that you wrote and published in Tvář called "Notes on
Quasi-Education." There you say: "Values that were genuinely world values in our country have always—and probably
more here than anywhere else—established themselves not in
harmony with our own domestic cultural qualities, but far
more often in opposition to them." You make the point using
Mácha, Hašek, Kafka, Janáček, and today I could probably
add Milan Kundera to the list as well.*

Of course you could, if that's how it seems to you. Personally, I don't think Kundera is such an outsider in Czech culture. For years he was the darling of his readership, and to
this day everyone knows who he is. When he was young, he
was decorated with the highest state prize for literature, and
if his books could be published here, the sales figures would
undoubtedly parallel those in the West. As far as the article
you quote is concerned, I would only add that today—thirty
years after it was written—I would operate somewhat more
cautiously with the notion of "world-class-ness." For me it has
lost its substance, just as the word "socialism" has.

In an anthology of your texts from the years 1969–79 called
On Human Identity, *there is an excerpt from the polemic
you had with Milan Kundera in 1968 and 1969. What's
missing, however, is Kundera's reply, published in* Host do
Domu *called "Radicalism and Exhibitionism," in which
Kundera argues against your point of view. Kundera was
always a defender and a supporter of victory or successful
compromises, and he is sarcastic about those who believe that*

"the defeat of just causes illuminates, with the light of an explosion, the entire misery of the world, the entire glory of the author's character." By leaving his part of the polemic out, doesn't it seem as though you have avoided the question he puts?

In the first place, the book you refer to was edited by Vilém Prečan and Alexander Tomský when I was in prison, which means that they, and not I, chose what was to be included. In the second place, their selection has a logic of its own. After all, it's an anthology of my work, and insofar as there are texts by other authors, there are only those to which I responded polemically, not those in which others responded to my points of view. In the third place, I am not avoiding the question you posed. I am quite familiar with Kundera's *(a priori)* skepticism regarding civic actions that have no immediate hope of being effective, and which therefore may appear to be no more than an attempt by their authors to show how wonderful they are, and I do not share that skepticism. In *The Unbearable Lightness of Being* there's a scene in which Tomáš' son asks his father to sign a petition in support of political prisoners; the father refuses to sign, and justifies his decision in the following way: The petition will not help the political prisoners, and as a matter of fact that's not why it was drawn up in the first place. Above all, it's a way for the authors to draw attention to themselves and to reassure themselves that they can still have an impact on history, whereas in fact they're doing this in a situation in which they've lost everything, and are in fact risking nothing at all by circulating the petition. Instead of the less conspicuous but more effective course of trying to aid the families of those prisoners, they are in fact parasites on the prisoners' misery, and through them are building a monument to themselves without taking into account that this may make things worse for the prisoners.

From the point of view of the novel, it's not important what particular petition inspired that episode and whether the petition was pointless or not. But I don't want to talk about the novel at all, I want to talk about reality. All the circumstances clearly indicate that Kundera was inspired by the first large writers' petition circulated after the period of "normalization" had begun, and that Tomáš is more or less a vehicle for Kundera's own point of view (which is also confirmed by the quote you mentioned). I remember that petition very well; I helped to gather signatures for it. It was very polite and cautious, nor did it question the sentences that were handed down; it merely appealed to the president's generosity and asked him to include the prisoners in the Christmas amnesty. (By the way, I don't think any Chartist would sign such a petition today, because of its compromising tone.) At the time, writers had not yet been sharply divided into those who were banned and those who were permitted to publish, and it wasn't clear yet which of them would sign the petition and which would not. In fact, some signed it who today are considered official writers. But it was the first significant act of solidarity in the Husák era, and therefore was something quite new.

The powers that be were very hostile to the petition, and several of those who signed immediately withdrew their signatures as soon as this hostility became clear. All those who did not sign or who withdrew their signatures argued in ways similar to Tomáš in Kundera's novel. They said they couldn't help anyone this way, that it would only annoy the government, that those who had already been banned were being exhibitionistic, and, worse, that through this petition, they were trying to drag those who still had their heads above water down into their own abyss by misusing their charity. Naturally the president did not grant an amnesty, and so Jaroslav Šabata, Milan Hübl, and others went on languishing in prison, while the beauty of our characters was illuminated. It would seem, therefore, that history proved our critics to be correct.

But was that really the case? I would say not. When the prisoners began to come back after their years in prison, they all said that the petition had given them a great deal of satisfaction. Because of it, they felt that their stay in prison had a meaning: it helped renew the broken solidarity. They knew, better than those of us who were outside, that the petition's significance transcended the question of whether or not they would be released—because they knew that they would not be released. But knowing that people knew about them, that someone was on their side and did not hesitate to support them publicly, even in a period of general apathy and resignation: this was of irreplaceable value. If for no other reason, that petition was important because of such feelings. (From my own experience, I know that news of people outside expressing their solidarity with him helps a person survive in prison.)

But it had a far deeper significance as well: it marked the beginning of a process in which people's civic backbones began to straighten again. This was a forerunner of Charter 77 and of everything the Charter now does, and the process has had undeniable results. Since that time, there have been hundreds of petitions, and although the government has reacted to none of them, it has had to respond to the changed situation which this endless flow of demands ultimately created. These results are indirect, modest, and long-range. But they exist. Here's one example: In the early seventies, prisoners were given long sentences for nothing, and almost no one, either at home or abroad, paid any attention, which was why the government could get away with such sentences. Today, after fifteen years of antlike work that often seemed Don Quixote–ish, and regardless of the continuing suspicion that the petitioners were merely exhibitionists who wished to illuminate "the entire misery of the world" and the glory of their own characters, all that has changed. Now all the authorities have to do is lock someone up for forty-eight hours for political reasons and newspapers all over the world write about it. In other words, international interest has been aroused, and the government has to take this interest into account. It can't get away with the sort of thing it used to get away with. It can no longer expect that no one will see what it is doing, or that no one will dare criticize it. It must—though it may not want to—reckon with the phenomenon of its own shame.

This, of course, has wider consequences, Today far more is possible. Think of this: hundreds of people today are doing things that not a single one of them would have dared to do at the beginning of the seventies. We are now living in a truly new and different situation. This is not because the government has become more tolerant; it has simply had to get used to the new situation. It has had to yield to continuing pressure from below, which means pressure from all those apparently suicidal or exhibitionistic civic acts. People who are used to seeing society only "from above" tend to be impatient. They want to see immediate results. Anything that does not produce immediately results seems foolish. They don't have a lot of sympathy for acts which can only be evaluated years after they take place, which are motivated by moral factors, and which therefore run the risk of never accomplishing anything. (In the article you refer to, Kundera took me to task for talking so much about risk—I believe he even counted the number of times I used the word. Yes, I used it frequently— it's a stylistic fault that I'm ashamed of—but I'm not ashamed of having drawn attention to the fact that risk is a lack of *a priori* assurance of success.) Unfortunately, we live in conditions where improvement is often achieved by actions that risk remaining forever in the memory of humanity in the form that the petition in *The Unbearable Lightness of Being* took: an exhibitionistic act of desperate people.

I don't want to do Kundera an injustice, but I can't avoid feeling that his notion of a Europe pillaged by Asia, his image of the spiritual graveyard, his idea that amnesia rules history and that history is an inexhaustible source of cruel jokes, all this lends support to the notion that nothing has changed in Czechoslovakia since the beginning of the 1970s, that all those petitions are as hopeless and absurd as they ever were, that they are even more clearly the desperate acts of lost souls who are trying to draw attention to themselves in a way that is tragically empty of meaning.

Naturally there may be a little of what Kundera is ridiculing in every petition and perhaps even in every signature. That is why I can't hold his ridicule against him, especially since it was in a novel. What I hold against him is something else: that he does not see, or willfully refuses to see, the other side of all those things, those aspects that are less obvious, more hidden, but more hopeful as well. I mean the indirect and long-term significance that these things can or may have. Kundera may be something of a prisoner of his own skepticism, because it does not allow him to admit that it occasionally makes sense to risk appearing ridiculous and act bravely. I can understand his terror of appearing ridiculous and of pathos, particularly given the enormous lesson he must have learned from his personal experience of communism. But I think this fear prevents him from perceiving the mysterious ambiguity of human behavior in totalitarian conditions. Complete skepticism is a psychologically understandable consequence of discovering that one's enthusiasms were based on illusion. But it can just as easily become the other side of the same false coin, and thus hide a more hopeful dimension to things—or, to put it more modestly, of the ambiguity of things.

At the risk of oversimplifying, perhaps we could summarize the reservations Czech intellectuals have about Kundera in a single sentence: Kundera's success has been bought at the price of going too far toward emulating the image that the West already has of the East. Even his belittling of those "protests" is something the West might like to hear in order to justify its frequently lukewarm support for such protests. Kundera, if I may quote him, would reply that we expect too much of the West all at once, that this makes us incomprehensible to the West so that we don't communicate anything at all, or only very little, and then only to a tiny circle of people.

You may find this disappointing, but now I must defend Kundera for a change. I don't believe that his main motive is simply a successful climb up the best-seller ladder, or that he is capable of trading in his convictions—under the guise of comprehensibility—for that success. I can't believe he would change his positions on protest or acts of solidarity in our part of the world simply because that is what he assumed the expectations of the Western readership were. That is simply how he sees these things, and he would obviously see them that way even if he were living here and didn't have to worry about the Western book market. In any case, his opinion is his own affair, and the fact that I have a rather different opinion means only that this is just the way it is.

It will soon be a hundred years since Gordon Hubert Schauer posed to the Czech nation a question to which we occasionally return. Most recently we were forcefully reminded of it in 1967, at a writers' congress, by Milan Kundera. I'd like to quote it now in its original version as it appeared in the magazine Čas (Time) *on December 20, 1886: "What is the role of our nation? What is our role in the history of mankind? What is the nature of our national existence? Are we as secure in our own house as we think we are? Is our national existence really worth the effort? Is its cultural value really so enormous? Are our national reserves so rich that they can provide sufficient moral strength to those who struggle for the nation* in extremis?" *How would you answer these questions today, and are these questions still worth asking at all?*

Personally, I don't bother myself with such questions. To me, my Czechness is a given, along with the fact that I am a man, or that I have fair hair, or that I live in the twentieth century. If I had lived during the national revival in the nineteenth century, my Czechness might still have been a matter of personal choice, and I might have tormented myself with the question of whether it was "worth the effort." The problem of whether we should develop the nation or simply give up on it is not something that I have to solve. These matters have already been decided by others. In any case, I have other worries. And the main worry is one common to all people everywhere: how to deal with one's life, how to bear and sort out one's dilemmas, whether they be human, existential, moral, or civic. The fact that I happen to have these dilemmas as a Czech living in Bohemia and not as an Argentinian living in Argentina is obviously related to the fact that—as Švejk says—we are all from somewhere; and for some reason or other the good Lord decided that I should vex the world and myself here and not in Argentina. In other words, I do not feel our Czechness as a burning or acute problem, and it seems to me that, if our national fate depends on anything, then it depends chiefly on how we acquit ourselves in our human tasks.

Here perhaps I should return to my old polemic with Milan Kundera, which you yourself raised, because it touched on precisely the question of our Czechness and our national destiny.

At the time, it bothered me that Kundera—and he was far from being the only one—began to explain the Soviet occupation and the Czechoslovak accommodation to it as part of our national lot, as though the Soviets had come here not to renew their version of order in a disobedient dominion but simply to fulfill the ancient Czech destiny, and as though for the same reason the representatives of our state had to sign the Moscow protocols. What was really a consequence of these events—Czech destiny or fate—was presented as their cause. I have nothing against historical parallels and meditations on the tendencies of our national history; it only bothers me when they are used to distract our attention from the living, human, moral and political dilemmas of the time, for, if we were to solve or deal with these, we would be making our own national history and ultimately giving it some kind of meaning. I full understand and respect the frustration of former communists with things as they have turned out. I don't like it when they cushion their landing on the hard truth by referring to an ancient national fate and thus, in the strict sense, wash their hands of it, as if history itself had to bear the responsibility for history!

There is something of this historical alibi in Kundera's writing to this day. As someone who once thought that he "had the steering wheel of history firmly in his hand" and who then, with great bitterness, realized that history was heading in another direction, he concluded from that—by a rather short circuit—that no one at all was holding the steering wheel of history. That was the source of his dehumanization of history; as though, from age to age, history were drifting somewhere high above us in a kind of fatal superworld, as though it were taking its own course, which had nothing to do with us and was utterly impenetrable, as though history were a clever divinity that could only destroy us, cheat us, misuse us, or—at best—play jokes on us. This, to me, is an excessive extrapolation of his own disillusionment. History is not something that takes place "elsewhere"; it takes place here; we all contribute to making it—Kundera through his novels, you with your interviews, the Chartists with their petitions. The good and the bad things that we do each day are a constituant part of that history. Life does not take place outside history, and history is not outside of life.

But back to the Czech question: I'm not saying the question doesn't exist. I would only recommend that we not treat it like a universal coatrack on which to hang all of life's unpleasantness, or as an abstract demon that can be blamed for all our particular human troubles. I've seen the "Czech question" play this role too often not to want to pay very careful attention to it when I am required to say something about it.

Do you see a grain of hope anywhere in the 1980s?

I should probably say first that the kind of hope I often think about (especially in situations that are particularly hopeless, such as prison) I understand above all as a state of mind, not a state of the world. Either we have hope within us or we don't; it is a dimension of the soul, and it's not essentially dependent on some particular observation of the world or estimate of the situation. Hope is not prognostication. It is an orientation of the spirit, an orientation of the heart; it transcends the world that is immediately experienced, and is anchored somewhere beyond its horizons. I don't think you can explain it as a mere derivative of something here, of some movement, or of some favorable signs in the world. I feel that its deepest roots are in the transcendental, just as the roots of human responsibility are, though of course I can't—unlike Christians, for instance—say anything concrete about the transcendental. An individual may affirm or deny that his hope is so rooted, but this does nothing to change my conviction (which is more than just a conviction; it's an inner experience). The most convinced materialist and atheist may have more of this genuine, transcendentally rooted inner hope (this is my view, not his) than ten metaphysicians together.

Hope, in this deep and powerful sense, is not the same as joy that things are going well, or willingness to invest in enterprises that are obviously headed for early success, but, rather, an ability to work for something because it is good, not just because it stands a chance to succeed. The more unpropitious the situation in which we demonstrate hope, the deeper that hope is. Hope is definitely not the same thing as optimism. It is not the conviction that something will turn out well, but the certainty that something makes sense, regardless of how it turns out. In short, I think that the deepest and most important form of hope, the only one that can keep us above water and urge us to good works, and the only true source of the breathtaking dimension of the human spirit and its efforts, is something we get, as it were, from "elsewhere." It is also this hope, above all, which gives us the strength to live and continually to try new things, even in conditions that seem as hopeless as ours do, here and now.

That was by way of introduction; now to answer your question about the state of the world and the kind of hopeful phenomena I see in it. Here too, I think, you can find modest grounds for hope. I leave it to those more qualified to decide what can be expected from Gorbachev and, in general, "from above"—that is, from what is happening in the sphere of power. I have never fixed my hopes there; I've always been more interested in what was happening "below," in what could be expected from "below," what could be won there, and what defended. All power is power over someone, and it always somehow responds, usually unwittingly rather than deliberately, to the state of mind and the behavior of those it rules over. One can always find in the behavior of power a reflection of what is going on "below." No one can govern in a vacuum. The exercise of power is determined by thousands of interactions between the world of the powerful and that of the powerless, all the more so because these worlds are never divided by a sharp line: everyone has a small part of himself in both.

Having said that, if I try to look unbiasedly at what is going on "below," I must say that here too I find a slow, imperceptible, yet undoubted and undoubtedly hopeful movement. After seventeen years of apparent stagnation and moribundity, the situation is rather different now. If we compare how society behaves now, how it expresses itself, what it dares to do—or, rather, what a significant minority dares to do—with how it was in the early seventies, those differences must be obvious. People seem to be recovering gradually, walking straighter, taking a renewed interest in things they had so energetically denied themselves before. New islands of self-awareness and self-liberation are appearing, and the connections between them, which were once so brutally disrupted, are multiplying. A new generation, not traumatized by the shock of the Soviet occupation, is maturing: for them, the invasion is history and Dubček is what Kramář, for example, was to my generation. Something is happening in the social awareness, though it is still an undercurrent as yet, rather than something visible.

And all of this brings subtle pressure to bear on the powers that govern society. I'm not thinking now of the obvious pressure of public criticism coming from dissidents, but of the invisible kinds of pressure brought on by this general state of mind and its various forms of expression, to which power unintentionally adapts, even in the act of opposing it. One is made aware of these things with special clarity when one returns from prison and experiences the sharp contrast between the situation as he had fixed it in his mind before his arrest, and the new situation at the moment of his return. I have observed this in my own case, and others have had the same experience. Again and again, we were astonished at all the new things that were going on, the greater risks people were taking, how much more freely they were behaving, how much greater and less hidden was their hunger for truth, for a truthful word, for genuine values. Just take the unstoppable development of independent culture: ten years ago there were no samizdat periodicals, and the idea of starting one would have been considered suicidal; today there are dozens of them, and people who were, until recently, famous for their caution are now contributing to them. Think of all the new samizdat books and publishing ventures; think of how many anonymous and improbable people are copying them out and distributing them; think of all the attention this is enjoying with the public! It bears no comparison whatever with the early seventies. But, then, think of all the new things in the sphere of public or permissible culture, or, rather, on its margins, in that vital gray belt or gray zone between official and independent cultures, where these spheres, which until very recently were so sharply divided, are now beginning to mix and mingle. If you were to find yourself at a concert of some young singer and songwriter or a nonconformist band, or in the audience of one of those new small theatres that are springing up everywhere, you would feel that the young people you see there live in their own world, a world very different from the one that breathes on us from the newspapers, from TV and the Prague radio. These two worlds simply fail to connect, and in a way that is far more basic and radical than analogous activity in the sixties which failed to connect with the ideology then. Whenever they say something about me on foreign radio, it is noticed by a far broader public than would ever notice an attack on me in *Tvorba*, the party cultural weekly.

It's not just that there now exists, as there did not ten years ago, an instrument—in Charter 77—for constantly monitoring power. There are other phenomena as well: the Jazz Section, for example, seems to me a model of its kind. The Jazz Section is not in any way deliberately oppositional or dissident; it certainly did not arise as a conscious act of political confrontation. The people in it are simply doing their work well; in other words, they are doing what everyone, theoretically, could do. The regime felt threatened and indirectly condemned by the Jazz Section's inner energy, by its departure from the cultural line, by its intellectual freedom, and moreover felt that it represented a scandalous flaw in the system of general manipulation. And so the regime started going after the Jazz Section, but the Section did not give in, and for three years now it has been leading a courageous struggle for its existence—and this was an organization that was originally a part of the official structures! It reminds me a little of the old story of *Tvář* that I've already talked about. Here again there is a precedent for a challenging new model of behavior. Of course there are more such examples, on many different levels and from many different areas of society. Until very recently, something like that would have been unthinkable.

Or take the rapid awakening and spread of religious feeling among young people, illustrated, for example, by the pilgrimmage in Velehrad. This is not an accidental phenomenon; it is an inevitable one: the endless, unchanging wasteland of the herd life in a socialist consumer society, its intellectual and spiritual vacuity, its moral sterility, necessarily causes young people to turn their attentions somewhere further and higher; it compels them to ask questions about the meaning of life, to look for a more meaningful system of values and standards, to seek, among the diffuse and fragmented world of frenzied consumerism (where goods are hard to come by) for a point that will hold firm—all this awakens in them a longing for a genuine moral "vanishing point," for something purer and more authentic. These people simply long to step outside the general automatic operations of society and rediscover their natural world and discover hope for this world. Against the "eschatology of the impersonal" they simply place another eschatology.

But things are different now from the way they were a few years ago, right in the midst of the so-called dissident or Chartist milieu as well. And although those in power have not altered their view of the Charter, they have still had to get used to it. Today it is a firm part of social life here, even though its position is marginal, one that society perceives more as the final horizon of its relationships or the final focus of various values than as an immediate challenge, something to be emulated. Today it is hard to imagine a time when the Charter did not exist, and when one does try to imagine it, it evokes a feeling of vacuum and moral relativity.

Or take VONS. A few of us were arrested and sent to prison for working in this "antistate center." When that happened, VONS did not cave in; others immediately filled in and continued the work. We didn't cave in either; we served our sentences, and VONS is here to this day, working energetically on, and apparently no one thinks anymore of prosecuting it for what it does. It still officially remains an "antistate organization" (an epithet those in power are too vainglorious to withdraw), but by insisting on it, they have turned it into a worthless phrase: what kind of an "antistate organization" is it that can go on publicly functioning for nine years? In a sense, our jail sentences gained us the right to run VONS.

To outside observers, these changes may seem insignificant. Where are your ten-million-strong trade unions? they may ask. Where are your members of parliament? Why does Husák not negotiate with you? Why is the government not considering your proposals and acting on them? But for someone from here who is not completely indifferent, these are far from insignificant changes; they are the main promise of the future, since he has long ago learned not to expect it from anywhere else.

I can't resist concluding with a question of my own. Isn't the reward of all those small but hopeful signs of movement this deep, inner hope that is not dependent on prognoses, and which was the primordial point of departure in this unequal struggle? Would so many of those small hopes have "come out" if there had not been this great hope "within," this hope without which it is impossible to live in dignity and meaning, much less find the will for the "hopeless enterprise" which stands at the beginning of most good things?

All your life you have stood up for writers, musicians, believers who were being discriminated against. Does this radical attitude toward discrimination come from your own experience of discrimination, or from some abstract philosophical conviction that freedom is indivisible?

As a matter of fact, I have never felt particularly discriminated against. I don't think I've ever suffered from a feeling that I've been singled out for abuse. I've always taken any discrimination against me in a sporting spirit, as a part of my life and an experience that can be used or—later—as a consequence of my own choice. So my experience of discrimination couldn't very well have been a conscious motive for expressing solidarity with others; though of course I don't know what subconscious influence it might have had.

Nor did I do such things out of theoretical conviction. For me it was always something that went without saying—in other words, something that was not dependent on my life or my philosophical opinions. To the extent that I ever thought about what compels me to such acts, it was always retrospectively. And if one of the basic themes of my letters from prison is the question "Why does one try to behave responsibly?" then the conclusion I came to is only a reflection of my experience with myself, and not an intellectual enlightenment so powerful that it would be enough, in itself, to drive me to certain practical actions.

A slightly different question: have you ever thought seriously about committing suicide? In your letters from prison, you reject the idea, of course, but that means that you must have at least considered it. Is suicide a solution?

Is there anyone who has never thought of suicide? Of course I've thought about it—many times—and in fact I still do, but probably only the way everyone who is capable of thought thinks about it. I think of it, for example, as a rope constantly stretched above me, which I can grab whenever I don't have the strength to go on. If I ever do grab it, it will be my final and definitive act, which of course will definitively rid me not only of life's woes, but of its joys as well. Personally, I'm still capable of living, and I don't have to grab the rope: I have never yet attempted suicide, and it doesn't seem likely that I will try it in the near future. On the contrary, I wish to try to go on living, despite everything. Paradoxically, this is something made possible by the possibility of suicide: knowing that one can always do it gives one the strength never to try it. Isn't life a kind of permanent deferral of suicide until later?

I can't answer the question about whether suicide is a solution or not. For those who have killed themselves, it obviously was. True, it is a rather abrupt solution—but perhaps it only seems that way to those of us who have not taken our own lives. But what do we know about it? Do we have any right at all to take such a high and mighty attitude to something we haven't known? (By this I don't mean the act of suicide itself, but the particular grief that came before it, the depth of the suicide's unhappiness, the depth of his inability to live with this unhappiness.)

In prison, I often had to dissuade fellow prisoners from committing suicide; I considered this my duty, and I would have had a heavy conscience indeed if someone had committed suicide whom I could have persuaded not to. (I once spent two weeks in "the hole" for attempting to stop someone from killing himself; our half-crazed warden yelled at me that I wasn't to interfere in the running of his camp.) But, to be frank, the arguments I used on such occasions would probably not have persuaded me if I were on the other end of them. It is really difficult to say why a person should live. Of course: we did not give ourselves life, so we have no right to take it away. But what if someone replies that he never asked God for it in the first place? And what if he tells you that it's all the same to him who gave him life, it's he who has to live it, and not the one who gave it to him. Or if he replies that, if God gave him life, he forgot to give him the strength of character to bear it? Fortunately, in such situations the decisive element is not the strength of the arguments but simply the will to live—and often one can impart that to someone else with the silliest of arguments.

So it's entirely possible that, if I were to run out of breath myself, I too might be saved by some clever but "silly" arguments. Be that as it may, I have never been able to condemn suicides; instead, I tend to respect them, not only for the undoubted courage needed to commit suicide, but also because suicides—in a certain sense—place the worth of life very high: they think that life is too precious a thing to permit its devaluation by living pointlessly, emptily, without meaning, without love, without hope. Sometimes I wonder if suicides aren't in fact sad guardians of the meaning of life.

I've heard that you've converted to Catholicism. If this is true, does it mean you have had that mystical experience which you refer to in your letters from prison as the probable condition of genuine inner conversion?

It depends on how we understand conversion. As I understand it, I would prefer to say no, I haven't converted. I have certainly not become a practicing Catholic: I don't go to church regularly, I haven't been to confession (I mean the institutional variety) since childhood, I don't pray, and I don't cross myself when I *am* in church. I took part in secret masses in prison, but I didn't take communion. There are some things that I have felt since childhood: that there is a great mystery above me which is the focus of all meaning and the highest moral authority; that the event called the "world" has a deeper order and meaning, and therefore is more than just a cluster of improbable accidents; that in my own life I am reaching for something that goes far beyond me and the horizon of the world that I know; that in everything I do I touch eternity in a strange way. But I never gave any of this any coherent thought until I was in prison, where I tried to describe and analyze my fundamental experience of the world and of myself.

But that doesn't mean I've changed—and conversion, after all, *means* change. Perhaps I understand my Protestant and Catholic friends better today—I'm certainly in greater touch with them, which may be why some people think I have converted. But genuine conversion, as I understand it, would mean replacing an uncertain "something" with a completely unambiguous personal God, and fully, inwardly, to accept Christ as the Son of God, along with everything that that entails, including the liturgy. And I have not taken that step. I'm no longer so certain I have to have that mystical experience: some deeply devout friends of mine tell me they had no such experience, nor had any need of it for their faith or conversion.

Whatever the case may be, I consider myself a believer only in the sense in which I used the word in my letters: I believe that all of this—life and the universe—is not just "in and of itself." I believe that nothing disappears forever, and less so our deeds, which is why I believe that it makes sense to try to do something in life, something more than that which will bring one obvious returns. But a lot of people could fit inside a faith so defined, and I don't suppose it would be responsible (and not even the most progressive theologians do it) to consider all such people believing Christians. I can try to live in the spirit of Christian morality (not very successfully, it's true), but that doesn't mean that I'm a genuinely believing Christian. I'm just not certain that Christ is the Son of God and a god-man, not just figuratively (as a kind of archetype of man), but in the profound and binding way that it holds true for a Christian.

You've already mentioned your plays. What else have you written?

Since early youth I've been writing articles, meditations, essays. The oldest ones, from the fifties, were never published (and I wouldn't want them to be). I have them at home, gathered into typewritten booklets. Among them, for instance, is a fairly long essay on Hrabal, written at a time when his books existed only in manuscript; it may be the very first analysis of his work. In the sixties I regularly published essays on theatre, profiles of actors and directors, and more general articles on art; this was largely for *Divadlo,* the theatre review. Besides that, I wrote a lot of different articles for theatre programs or art catalogues, introductions, and afterwords—brief articles. If I were required to find all of it and put it together, I don't think I could do it.

I've already mentioned a book called *Protocols,* put out by Mlada Fronta; that book contained "Anticodes," a collection of my typographical poems. My essays, articles, feuilletons, and various pieces of writing from the seventies are collected in a book called *On Human Identity* (Rozmluvy, London, 1984). The most extensive and most important essay in it is probably "The Power of the Powerless," written in 1978. I've also talked about *Letters to Olga* (first published by 68 Publishers in Toronto), a collection of my letters from prison. The final cycle of letters was also published separately, under the title *An Invitation to Transcendence* (Rozmluvy, London, 1984), together with a remarkable study by "Sidonius." There are already quite a few articles written after my return from prison, such as "Politics and Conscience," "Responsibility as Destiny," "Thriller," "The Anatomy of a Reticence," to name a few of the more important ones. An extensive interview I gave to foreign reporters shortly after getting out of prison is very important, personally (it was published in Czech as a supplement to *Listy*). Perhaps all these pieces will one day be collected in a book.

Have I forgotten anything? There's my thesis for AMU (an analysis of my own play *The Increased Difficulty of Concentration*), and the sixty-page commentary on *The Conspirators* from the early seventies, which is, in fact, a rather detailed disquisition on the theme of human identity. I think this was the first time I put a name to my basic dramatic theme, and the commentary is probably better than the play. Finally, for the sake of completeness, I should mention that I have written, or co-written countless collective position papers, declarations, documents, and the like, mainly after the appearance of Charter 77.

How would you describe the aesthetics or the poetics of your plays? What, in your opinion, do they all share in common, and how would you characterize yourself as a playwright?

To answer this question properly, I'd have to step beyond myself for a while and look at myself objectively, which is not an easy task. Still, I will try, with the proviso that my self-portrait will be a rather rough sketch, limited to a few of the most obvious features, as I see them myself.

I'll start with the externals. It would be hard to find in my plays a subtle thread of atmosphere or mood, or a wide range of finely nuanced psychological situations or glimpses into the secret and complex motions of the human mind and soul. You will find that their interior structure, the way they're put together, is not very cleverly disguised, nor do they appear to be a spontaneous, smooth-flowing, natural unfolding of life in a series of incidents. I'm the type of author who constructs his plays, and I admit it; I deliberately make their structures easy to grasp, I stress them, reveal them, and often give them geometrically direct and regular features—all in the hope that it will not be understood as a clumsy fault, or as something deliberately self-serving, but as something that has a certain meaning as well.

As I've already said in another connection, I don't have a musical ear, and I certainly don't have a wide knowledge of music, but I still think that, because of this intensified emphasis on composition, something close to music and musical thought enters my plays. I really enjoy things like the symmetrical—and ultimately the symmetrically asymmetrical—interweaving and mingling of motifs, phasing them in and out, developing them rhythmically, mirroring motifs in their opposites. Again and again I find myself tending toward the analogical construction of dialogue: recapitulating bits of dialogue, repeating them, interchanging them, putting words spoken by one character in the mouth of another and then back again, dialogue running backward or contradicting itself, stressing the rhythmic alternation of conversational themes, which again means stressing the time element. All of this, to a greater or lesser degree, can be found in my plays. In one of them—*Mountain Hotel*—I have even tried to develop these techniques to the point where they become the theme of the play; in other words, *Mountain Hotel* was, in a sense, a play about itself, which of course had—or more precisely, should have had—its own "meta-meaning."

So at first glance you can tell that my plays are con-
sciously, deliberately, and obviously constructed, schematic,
almost machinelike. This is not because sometime at the beginning of my writing career I made a cold-blooded decision
to write in this eccentric fashion and no other. Rather, it came
out of my proper tendencies and interests, out of my nature.
There are various scholarly ways the meaning of these matters
can be explained. For instance, they might be seen as an attempt to demonstrate clearly the inner mechanism of certain
social and psychological processes, and the mechanical nature of how man is manipulated in the modern world, which
is in turn related to the scientific and ultimately the techno-
logical origin of this manipulation. I have nothing against
such interpretations; they are legitimate, and there is no doubt
something to them. I would only add, again, that at the beginning I had no intention, for whatever "ideological" reasons,
to write in a particular way. It's not as simple as that. The fact
is that particular authors, by their very nature, are drawn in
a particular direction, and through the thing they are drawn
to they touch something else—or, rather, the thing they are
drawn to leads them to something else itself. Everything of
value always means more than the author intended.

Another thing I should mention here is an interest in language. I'm interested in its ambivalence, its abuse; I'm interested in language as something that fashions life, destinies,
and worlds; language as the most important skill; language as
ritual and magic charm; the word as a carrier of dramatic
movement, as something that legitimizes, as a way of self-
affirmation and self-projection. I am interested in clichés and
their meaning in a world where verbal evaluation, inclusion
in a phraseological context, linguistic interpretation are often
more important than reality itself, and "real reality" merely
derives from clichés. Someone wrote that the main hero of
The Garden Party is the cliché. The cliché organizes life; it
expropriates people's identity; it becomes ruler, defense lawyer, judge, and the law. I enjoy writing rhetorical speeches in
which nonsense is defended with crystal-clear logic. I enjoy

writing monologues in which pure truths are expressed with veracity and subtlety, truths which are pure lies from beginning to end. Even more, I enjoy writing speeches that balance on a knife's edge: the audience members identify with the truths expressed in them, yet they sense a scarcely perceptible tinge of mendacity, given the situation and context, and they become uneasy, wondering how it was all meant. In *Temptation,* for example, Foustka expounds his opinions on the basic questions of being to Marketa, and in doing so he tells her things that are almost identical to what I believe myself and what, in similar words and in all seriousness, I have said elsewhere, such as in my letters from prison, or in this conversation. At the same time, there is something subtly false in what Foustka says. He says it—and this is something we should not miss—partly because he is trying to get Marketa to fall in love with him, and he succeeds. So he is, be it ever so subtly, abusing his own truth, one that he has, by honorable means, arrived at himself.

But is it still truth, then? Isn't just such a subtle abuse of the truth, and of language, the real beginning of Foustka's misery, and of the misery of the world we live in? The audience should not be entirely clear about these things; the ambivalence should disquiet them, all the more so because from their own experience—that is, if they are men—they would know that we are often at our most eloquent in formulating important truths when we set out to charm women with them. I remember when *The Memorandum* was being performed. The main character, in his final speech, defends his own moral degradation by appealing to the general absurdity of the world and to alienation, which he expressed in the then freshly rediscovered jargon of existentialism. Someone asked me how I'd really meant it—that is, whether I'd seriously meant to defend his moral degradation, or whether I had intended, by making fun of that kind of talk, to distance myself from modern philosophy's revival of Marxism. The person concerned was upset, and I couldn't have asked for a better response. A cliché is always a cliché; there are no "progressive" clichés or "reactionary" clichés; the more "progressive" a phrase is, the less it appears to be a cliché, the more it interests me.

The mechanization of dramatic forms in my work may actually be the most important aesthetic quality of those plays. Taken all together, my plays are based not so much on the behavior of the characters and the movement of events as they are on movements of meanings, motifs, thoughts, signs, arguments, notions, theses, words. All of this seems to come alive and ultimately carries the real action, if it can still be called action, and is the real source of the drama. Of course, this inevitably means that my plays are full of signs, which are abbreviated and schematic. There is a little of the puppet show in them, something of the animated machine. More than one critic, or director, or actor has found the plays hard to come to terms with; they wanted more psychology, more of the color and juice of life; they wanted mystery, accident, irregularity. Everything seemed cold, calculated, written according to some graph, composed of generalizations; they felt there was no niche in them for mystery, miracle, the unexpected, hope, for the uniqueness of the living. I understood these people entirely, but at the same time, I stuck to my guns.

Perhaps I should ask myself what my plays are really about. Whether I want to or not, whether I plan it or not, one basic theme always gets into my plays, almost obsessively, and thus not by chance at all, but from the very essence of those aspects of the world that have chosen me as their interpreter— that is, the theme of human identity. It is a theme that is traditionally connected with theatre: ultimately, all theatre is built around the conflict between who a character seems to be and who he really is. The process of appearing, revealing, of recognizing the true face of a person can be found in all theatre, from antiquity until today. The question of identity is implicit in the phenomenon of masks, just as it is in that of disguise. In my plays, however, this intrinsically theatrical or dramatic theme comes back in a rather more special form: as the theme of identity in crisis. It is not just about identity hidden behind a mask, hypocrisy, or a social role, but identity that is decaying, collapsing, dissipating, vanishing.

The crisis is all the worse in that it is not reflected upon. In my first play, *The Garden Party*, the theme is projected directly into the subject: the main character, Hugo, goes into the world—something like Jack in the folk tales, who sets out to seek his fortune (the archetype of the pilgrim)—and he encounters the cliché as the central principle of that world. Gradually, he adapts to the cliché (he "learns"); he comes to identify with it; the more he identifies with it, the higher he rises; and when he is at the top, it turns out that he has entirely dissolved in clichés and thus has lost himself. The play ends with Hugo going to visit himself. He doesn't do this in order to find himself again, but in order to get closer to someone he considers extremely important. The fact that this person is himself is merely a "misunderstanding," albeit symbolic: he had heard of his own importance and, not realizing that the person was himself, set out to find himself. His fixation on the cliché brings him back to himself, as the cliché's highest embodiment. In the act of visiting himself, he definitively loses himself. In a variety of less obvious forms, the motif of loss of self crops up in all the rest of my plays.

What else can I say about them? Perhaps that they are in no way avant-garde. In this I am faithful to the tradition of the theatre of the absurd. The curtain opens, onstage there is a room with several doors (I love the mystery of doors, those borders of space, those mediators of entrances and exits, the gateways to theatrical being and nonbeing), someone comes in, says hello, and so on. There is no dragging the spectator onstage, or sending the actors into the audience, no sorcery, no stepping out of roles or anything like that, just a normal play, in which what happens proceeds from what came before. In the beginning are precise rules or conventions. It is only after these are established that the process of gradually overturning and undermining them can begin, of travestying and disrupting them, and disrupting their disruption, their abuse. I have always claimed that, where everything is permitted, nothing can surprise. Drama assumes an order. If only so that it might have—by disrupting that order—a way of surprising.

How would you respond to the objection you mentioned, that there is no transcendence in your plays, no room for mystery, for the multiplicity of life?

By comparing them with the visual arts, for one thing. Just imagine a surrealist or postsurrealist painting, something like that, that shows a subway station with a mysterious troll-like woman walking up and down the platform, a devil poking his chin out somewhere, broken eggs on the ground, an umbrella leaning against the wall. If the picture is good, something magical and mysterious will emanate from it; we will discover something of the dark and secret movements of our own psyche or unconsciousness. Looking at it, we will feel a slight shiver, because we sense the presence of our own archetypal imaginings. But these references to mystery, of course, are overtly thematical; they are in the subject itself; they are, as it were, directly painted.

But one could imagine another painting, let's say from op art or geometrical abstraction, where nothing overtly mysterious has been painted; there may be only a series of concentric circles, or colored squares; everything has its own clear order; there isn't a single anomaly in it that might raise questions. The picture seems to have no mystery to it; a computer might have painted it according to a set of programmed instructions; there is no view through it to somewhere beyond; the picture itself is superfluous, because the idea can be thought or expressed otherwise. I'm convinced that such a picture too—minus the melting watches and the cracked eggs—can have its own secret. But that secret lies somewhere in the subtext, in what is not in the picture, in the interstices between the circles, in the very composition of its elements, in the mystery of their meaning, in the question: What are they and what do they mean, and where did they come from? After all, isn't the very existence of those geometric elements a great mystery? Are they some primordial forms of being? Or primordial forms of our mind? Or of the mind of God? What are they doing here? What are they trying to tell us? Where did their order come from? Is it the order of creation, or the order of death? What is between those circles, or within them, behind them, around them? Nothing? Are they themselves something at all, or are they only another modality of the same nothing? Did a human spirit abstract them from the universe, or are they only its mad phantoms? What, in fact, is obsessing the person who painted this? What is he trying to tell us? Does he know anything special? Is it a message about the scope of Being, or an expression of pure despair? I could go on and on asking questions like that.

I think that every genuine work of art has some mystery in it, though this may only be in its structure, in the secret of its composition, the touch, the clash, or lack of clash, among the forms, in the mystery of those structural events. Every work of art points somewhere beyond itself; it transcends itself and its author; it creates a special force field around itself that moves the human mind and the human nervous system in a way that its author could scarcely have planned ahead of time. It is impossible to number the rays that emanate from it, and no one can see where they end. They grow weaker, of course, but they carry on to infinity. If I did not hope that my plays have something of those qualities, regardless of whom they may affect, I wouldn't have written them.

How would you reply to those who criticize your plays, and Temptation *in particular, for being thoroughly pessimistic, offering no way out, not a scrap of hope? Would you concede that the world of your plays is somewhat in conflict with your civic stance and your life?*

The role of theatre, as I understand it and as I have tried to practice it, is not to make people's lives easier by presenting positive heroes into which they can project all their hopes, and then sending them home with the feeling that these heroes will take care of things for them. To my mind, that would be doing the lion's share of the work. I've already talked about how each of us must find real, fundamental hope within himself. You can't delegate that to anyone else.

My ambition is not to soothe the viewer with a merciful lie or cheer him up with a false offer to sort things out for him. I wouldn't be helping him very much if I did. I'm trying to do something else: to propel him, in the most drastic possible way, into the depths of a question he should not, and cannot, avoid asking; to stick his nose into his own misery, into my misery, into our common misery, by way of reminding him that the time has come to do something about it. The only ways out, the only solutions, the only hopes that are worth anything are the ones we discover ourselves, within ourselves, and for ourselves. Perhaps with God's help. But theatre does not mediate that kind of help; it is not a church. Theatre ought to be—with God's help—theatre. And one way of helping people is by reminding them that the time is getting late, that the situation is grave, that it can't be ignored. Seeing the outlines of horror induces the will to face up to it. As Ivan Jirous wrote about *Temptation:* the hope in the play lies in the observation that you can't make a pact with the devil. But this is an observation the viewer must make himself—I can only help him to come to that conclusion by demonstrating what happens when you do make a pact with the devil. I repeat what Glucksmann said: our mission is to warn, to predict horrors, to see clearly what is evil. Face to face with a distillation of evil, man might well recognize what is good. By showing good on the stage, we ultimately rob him of the possibility of making such a recognition himself—as his own existential act.

In *Temptation*, Fistula says: "I don't give practical advice, and I don't make arrangements for anyone. At the most, I occasionally goad into action." That speech could be my credo as a writer. Everyone has to make his own arrangements, within himself. If I can goad someone into realizing, with heightened urgency, that there are some arrangements to be made, then I've done my job, which is to remind people of their dilemma, to stress the importance of questions that have been pushed aside and lost sight of, to demonstrate that there really is something to be settled here. Only the solutions a person discovers himself will be the proper ones. They will be his, they will be an act of his own creation and his self-creation.

You might object that there have been times when drama could not get by without great heroes and positive, if tragic, characters. Certainly. But those times are past. Drama, in a unique way, always mirrors what is essential in its time. This is not a time for great heroes, and if they appear, they are mendacious, ridiculous, and sentimental. This is not because playwrights have conspired to make it so. Ask the modern world why it is this way.

And a final thing. Most people don't know how to read plays. (And why should they? Wouldn't this render theatre redundant?) Among other things, they can't drop their private reader's experience and imagine the radically different collective experience of theatre. When you are in an audience, your experience is different from what it would be at home in an easy chair. When I was supervising performances of my own plays at the Theatre on the Balustrade, I could watch audiences' reactions very closely. Each time I did, I was reminded of how being in an audience gives everything another dimension. If you read a play in which evil is named, in which everything turns out badly, and in which there isn't a single positive character, you can easily be depressed by it, and little else. But if you see the play performed in a theatre, in that exciting atmosphere of common understanding, you suddenly feel completely different about it. Even the toughest truth expressed publicly, in front of everyone else, suddenly becomes liberating. In the beautiful ambivalence that is proper only to theatre, the horror of that truth (and why hide it—it looks worse onstage than it does when we read it) is wedded to something new and unfamiliar, at least from our reading: to delight (which can only be experienced collectively), because it was finally said, it's out of the bag, the truth has finally been articulated out loud and in public.

In the ambivalence of this experience there is something that has been a part of theatre from the beginning: catharsis. Jan Grossman once wrote of my plays that their positive hero is the audience. This doesn't just mean that a viewer who is moved by what he has seen may start looking for a real solution (not a generally transferable solution, like the answer to a crossword puzzle, but an untransferable act: his own existential awakening). It also means that he becomes this "positive hero" while he's still in the audience, as one who participates and cocreates the catharsis, sharing with others the liberating delight in evil exposed. Through the demonstration of the misery of the world, an experience is evoked that is—paradoxically—profoundly edifying. Somewhere in here is the beginning of hope—real hope, not hope for a happy ending. But if the play is truly to evoke this, it must somehow be internally disposed to do so. Horror per se, or just any kind of horror, doesn't automatically lead to catharsis. Some secret enzymes must be at work in the tissue of the play. But how to do it is my problem; let me be judged only by the results. The theatrical results, of course.

As for the conflict between the world of my plays and my civic activities, I've already dealt with this theme in my letters from prison, and I've touched on it in this conversation as well. So, to be brief: If I ignore the trivial truth that art operates by different rules from those of life or from those of thoughts conveyed through essays, I have to point again to the complementary nature of sense and nonsense. The deeper the experience of an absence of meaning—in other words, of absurdity—the more energetically meaning is sought; without a vital struggle with the experience of absurdity, there would be nothing to reach for; without a profound inner longing for sense, there could not then be any wounding by nonsense.

You've evaluated yourself as a playwright; how would you evaluate yourself as a person? You're approaching fifty now; perhaps this might be an occasion for some self-reflection as well—

It's a diabolical task, and the first and only thing I can say about it right now is that my life, my work, my position, everything I've done, seems intertwined with a suspiciously large number of paradoxes. Take this one, for instance: I get involved in many things, yet I'm an expert in none of them. Over the years, for example, I've become known as a political activist, but I've never been a politician, never wanted to be one; I don't have any of the necessary qualities for it. Both my opponents and my supporters see me as a political phenomenon, though nothing I do can be considered real politics. Every once in a while I philosophize—yet what kind of philosopher am I anyway? Certainly I've enjoyed reading philosophical books since my youth, but my philosophical education is more than shaky, and thoroughly piecemeal. I occasionally write about literature—yet, if there's anything I most certainly am not, it's a literary critic. There are times when I even stick my nose into music, and yet, if anything, my musicality is only a source of general amusement. Even in what I would consider my chief, original vocation—theatre— I'm not really an expert. I went through theatre school quickly and without much interest; I don't like reading plays or books on theatre; I don't enjoy going to most theatre; I have a personal opinion, of sorts, about the kind of theatre I like, and I write my plays in that spirit, but that's all.

So I'm not at all certain that theatre is my very own, unique and indispensable mission. I can easily imagine that, if an irresistible opportunity were to come my way, I could just as easily devote the same amount of energy to another discipline. I certainly don't feel like a professional theatre person, one inevitably drawn to theatre, whose destiny is forever linked with the theatre. And rather than be a dramaturge in any old theatre just because I've been trained to be one, I'd prefer to go back to working in a brewery. In any case, as a dramatist I'm somewhat suspect: I can write in my own highly particular way, within the limits of my narrowly defined poetics, but if I had to write something that even slightly departed from that, I would probably be a miserable failure.

In general, then, though I have a presence in many places, I don't really have a firm, predestined place anywhere, in terms of neither my employment, nor my expertise, nor my education and upbringing, nor my qualities and skills. I'm not saying that airborne, unrooted, disturbing existences such as mine are not necessary. But this alters nothing in the paradoxical tension between the seriousness with which I am accepted and my amateurism. The list of my private paradoxes doesn't end here, it's just the beginning. Some others, at random: I have chosen a rather agitated way of life, and I myself am always ruffling the surface somewhere, yet I long for nothing more than peace and quiet. I have an extraordinary love of harmony, comfort, agreement, and friendly mutual understanding between people (I'd be happiest if everyone simply liked everyone else, always); tension, conflict, misunderstanding, uncertainty, and confusion upset me; yet my position in the world always has been and continues to be deeply controversial. I've been in conflict with the state and with various institutions and organizations all my life; my reputation is that of an eternal rebel and protester, to whom nothing is sacred; and my plays are anything but a picture of peace and harmony. I'm very unsure of myself, almost a neurotic. I tend to panic easily; I'm always terrified of something, scared even that the telephone might ring; I'm plagued by self-doubts, and I'm always masochistically blaming or cursing myself for something; yet I appear to many (and to a degree rightly so!) as someone who is sure of himself, with an enviable equanimity, quiet, levelheaded, constant, persistent, down-to-earth, always standing up for himself. I am rational and systematic, I love order and orderliness; I am disciplined and reliable, at times almost bureaucratically pedantic; at the same time I'm oversensitive, almost a little sentimental, someone who's always been drawn by everything mysterious, magic, irrational, inexplicable, grotesque, and absurd, everything that escapes order and makes it problematic. I'm a sociable person who likes being with people, organizing events, bringing people together; a cheerful fellow, sometimes the conversational life of the party, one who enjoys drinking and the various pleasures and trespasses of life—and at the same time I'm happiest when alone, and consequently my life is a constant escape into solitude and quiet introspection.

You pointed to another paradox yourself a while ago, and even though I was able to show that it wasn't really a paradox, I admit that it must seem that way: I write mercilessly skeptical, even cruel plays—and yet in other matters I behave almost like a Don Quixote and an eternal dreamer, foolishly struggling for some ideal or another. At my core I'm shy and timid—and yet in some forums I'm notorious as a rabble-rouser who is not afraid to say the toughest things right to someone's face. Or something else, which I've already mentioned in another connection: for many people I'm a constant source of hope, and yet I'm always succumbing to depressions, uncertainties, and doubts, and I'm constantly having to look hard for my own inner hope and revive it, win it back from myself with great difficulty, so that I scarcely seem to have any to give away. So I'm not really comfortable in the role of a distributor of hope and encouragement to those around me, since I'm always on the lookout for some encouragement myself. I come across as one who is steadfast and brave, if not hardheaded, who did not hesitate to choose prison when far more attractive options were offered him— and there are times when I have to laugh at my reputation. The fact is, I'm always afraid of something, and even my alleged courage and stamina spring from fear: fear of my own conscience, which delights in tormenting me for real and imaginary failures. And all that heroic time in prison was in fact one long chain of worries, fears, and terrors: I was a frightened, terrified child, confusedly present on this earth, afraid of life, and eternally doubting the rightness of his place in the order of things; I probably bore prison worse than most of those who admired me would. Whenever I heard the familiar shout in the hallways, "Havel!," I would panic. Once, after hearing my name yelled out like that, I jumped out of bed without thinking and cracked my skull on the window. And with all this, and despite all this, I know that, if it were necessary, I would go back to prison again, and I would survive.

I could make a long list of such paradoxes, but my reluctance to talk about myself in public is gradually winning out over my good will in wishing to answer your questions truthfully, so I'll conclude with some questions that I sometimes ask myself: How does it all fit together? Why don't these paradoxical qualities cancel each other out instead of coexisting and cooperating with each other? What does all this mean? What should I think about it all? How can I—this odd mix of the most curious opposites—get through life, and by all reports successfully?

One final question. Given this awareness of yourself, how do you see your future? What do you think is awaiting you? What do you hope for, and what do you expect?

The paradoxes will continue. I'll go on, as I've always done, sitting down in front of a blank piece of paper with distaste; I will try everything to avoid writing, always terrified of those first words on the page. I will continue to find artificial ways of giving myself the courage to write. I will despair that it's not coming, yet I'll always manage to write a new play. The mysterious inner furies who have invented these torments will probably not leave me in peace and will have their own way in the end. As always, I will be upset by all the expectations (many of which are out of proportion and even foolish) that I'm burdened with, and all the roles, from the representative to the Good Samaritan, that are prescribed for me. I will continue to revolt against them and reclaim my right to peace—

and I will ultimately carry out all these tasks and even find sincere delight in doing so. I will go on being bothered by things, fearing some things, getting into states, blaming myself, cursing, and despairing—and, as always, I will be found reliable and will be seen where my place is. I'll always end up paying for it, but, oddly enough, I'll survive and be there, causing disruption wherever necessary.

I can only conclude this prediction, and our conversation, by attempting to articulate the final and obviously the most paradoxical paradox of my life: I suspect that somewhere, deep down, I find this paradoxical life of mine terribly entertaining.

Glossary

Havel has made many references that may be unfamiliar to readers. For reasons of space, I have identified only those names which are most relevant to understanding Havel's context.—P.W.

AMU. Akademie Muzických Umění (The Academy of Arts).

Auersperg, Pavel. Important figure in the Cultural section of the Central Committee of the Communist Party prior to the Prague Spring of 1968.

Bass, Eduard (1888–1946). Journalist, writer, editor-in-chief of *Lidové Noviny* (until 1945 known as *Svobodné Noviny*). *Umberto's Circus* (New York: Farrar & Straus, 1951).

Bělohradský, Václav (1944–). Philosopher, sociologist, professor at University of Genoa.

Benda, Václav (Vašek) (1946–). Philosopher and mathematician. "Catholicism and Politics" in *The Power of the Powerless,* Václav Havel et al. (Armonk, New York: M. E. Sharpe, 1985).

Beneš, Jan (1936–). Writer, resident in the United States. *The Blind Mirror* (New York: Grossman, 1971); *Second Breath* (New York: Orion, 1969).

Bilăk, Vasil. Politician, Slovak secretary of Communist Party; supported the Warsaw Pact invasion of 1968.

Cerný, Václav (1905–). Literary critic and theorist, until 1950 professor at Charles University. *Dostoevsky and the Devils* (Ann Arbor, Michigan: Ardis, 1975); "On the Question of Chartism" in *The Power of the Powerless*, Václav Havel, et al. (Armonk, New York: M. E. Sharpe, 1985).

Chalupecký, Jindřich (1910–). Art and literary critic, founding member of Group 42.

Charter 77. Readers wishing to know more about the origins and nature of Charter 77 should consult *Charter 77 and Human Rights in Czechoslovakia*, by H. Gordon Skilling. (London: George Allen & Unwin, 1981). In his Introduction, Skilling writes:

On 6 January 1977—Twelfth Night, or as it is called in Czechoslovakia, 'the day of the three kings'—a beaten-up white Saab, driven by Pavel Landovský, actor and playwright, was blocked in downtown Prague by a number of state security cars, and its three passengers were detained for questioning. In the back seat of the automobile were about 250 envelopes containing copies of a document which had been picked up at various houses during the morning. The three persons were not the three kings, Kašpar, Melichar and Baltazar, who according to Czech tradition, wear paper crowns on their heads and leave their initials in chalk on houses visited during their yearly journey through the city. They were, in addition to Landovský, the celebrated writers, Václav Havel, playwright, and Ludvík Vaculík, novelist, bound for the post-office to mail copies of Charter 77 to its 240 signatories, and to the government of Czechoslovakia, the Federal Assembly, and the Czechoslovak Press Agency (CTK). With a fourth person, Zdeněk Urbánek, also a writer, the three messengers spent Twelfth Night in detention, under interrogation by the security police, and were released shortly after midnight. Two others, František Pavlíček, another writer, and Jan Petránek, a journalist, were arrested the next day, and released a day later; so was Havel, who had been detained a second time. Charter 77, however, had reached its official destinations, although in an unexpected and strange manner. It was published in full, in German, the next day in the *Frankfurter Allgemeine Zeitung*, and appeared in many other newspapers throughout the world.

Chytilová, Věra. Movie director, film scenarist, best known for *Daisies*.

Glossary

Devětsil. An avant-garde, left-wing writers circle founded in Prague in the early 1920s. It was allied to the Communist Party and committed to revolution in life, art, and politics.

Dienstbier, Jiří (1937–). Journalist and former Czech radio correspondent in the Far East and the United States. Since December 1989, Foreign Minister of Czechoslovakia. *Reception* in *The Vaněk Plays*, Marketa Goetz-Stankiewicz, ed. (Vancouver: University of British Columbia Press, 1987).

Drda, Jan (1915–). Writer, journalist, film scenarist; editor-in-chief of *Lidové Noviny* (1948–52); head of the Union of Czechoslovak Writers (1949–56).

Drtina, Prokop (1900–1980). Minister of Justice until 1948, later imprisoned.

Eisner, Pavel (1889–1958). Writer and translator of Czech into and from German (works by Goethe, Schiller, Kleist, Heine, Rilke, Kafka, and others). Friend of Max Brod, Egon Kisch, Franz Werfel.

Fikar, Ladislav (1920–1975). Poet, translator, critic, from 1948 to 1959 editor-in-chief and managing director of Československý Spisovatel publishing house. Artistic director of Czech state film (1960–68), playing a part in the Czech New Wave of the 1960s.

Fischer, Josef Ludvík (1894–1973). Philosopher and sociologist, professor at universities of Brno and Olomouc.

Forman, Miloš (1936–). Film director, since 1968 resident in the United States, winner of numerous Oscars. Films include *Loves of a Blonde, The Fireman's Ball, One Flew Over the Cuckoo's Nest, Hair,* and *Amadeus.*

Glazarova, Jarmila (1901–). Writer with social realistic orientiation; cultural attaché in Moscow (1946–48); member of Czechoslovak parliament (1945–56).

Goldstücker, Eduard (1913–). Literary historian and Germanist.

Grossman, Jan (1925–). Literary critic and stage director.

Group 42. Group of avant-garde writers, poets, and artists founded in 1942.

Glossary

Gruša, Jiří (1933–). Poet and prose writer. *The Questionnaire* (New York: Farrar, Straus & Giroux, 1982); *Franz Kafka of Prague* (New York: Schocken, 1984); "A Bride for Sale," "Salamandra," and "The Feuilletons I Promised to Write," in *The Writing on the Wall*, Antonín Liehm and Peter Kussi, eds. (New York: Karz-Cohl, 1983). Lives in West Germany.

Hájek, Jiří (1913–). Czechoslovakia's foreign minister in 1968; earlier, ambassador to United States and United Nations. "An Attempt at a Feuilleton," in *The Writing on the Wall*, Antonín Liehm and Peter Kussi, eds. (New York: Karz-Cohl, 1983).

Hájek, Jiří (1919–). Marxist literary critic, editor-in-chief of *Plamen* (1960s) and *Tvorba* (1970s).

Hanč, Jan (1916–1963). Olympic athlete, represented Czechoslovakia in 1936. Poet, member of Group 42.

Hejdánek, Ladislav (1927–). Philosopher. "Prospects for Democracy and Socialism in Eastern Europe" in *The Power of the Powerless*, Václav Havel et al. (Armonk, New York: M. E. Sharpe, 1983).

Hiršal, Josef (1920–). Poet, wrote concrete and visual poetry, translator, author of works for children.

Holan, Vladimír (1905–1980). Poet. *A Night With Hamlet* (London: Oasis, 1980); *Selected Poems* (Hammondsworth: Penguin, 1971); various anthologies.

Horáková, Milada (1901–1950). National Assembly delegate for the Czech Socialist party, sentenced to death at show trial on June 8, 1950.

Horníček, Miroslav. Actor, comedian, monologuist of cabaret shows in the *Semafor* theatre in Prague.

Hrabal, Bohumil (1914–). Prose writer. *Closely Watched Trains* (New York: Grove, 1968); *The Death of Mr. Baltisberger* (Garden City: Doubleday, 1975); *I Served the King of England* (New York: Harcourt Brace Jovanovich, 1989); widely anthologized.

Hrubín, František (1910–). Poet, translator, author of poetry for children.

Glossary

Hübl, Milan (d. 1989). Historian and reform Communist; signatory of Charter 77 .

Hutka, Jaroslav (1947–). Underground singer, since 1978 resident in Western Europe. "The Dimensions of the Body," in *The Writing on the Wall*, Antonín Liehm and Peter Kussi, eds. (New York: Karz-Cohl, 1983).

Indra, Alois. Politician, member of Czechoslovak government and Communist Party Politburo; supported the Warsaw Pact invasion of Czechoslovakia in August 1968.

Jazz Section. An organization that began within the Czech Union of Musicians to promote jazz. In the late 1970s and early 1980s, it published magazines and books and arranged concerts for domestic and foreign groups. Though its activities remained centered on music, it encompassed all forms of popular culture. In 1987, after several years of mounting pressure from the authorities, its leaders were sent to prison and the organization was disbanded. See "Hipness at Noon," by Josef Škvorecký, in *The New Republic*, December 17, 1984, for more complete information.

Jirous, Ivan [pseudonym Magor] (1944–). Poet and visual arts historian. "New Art in Czechoslovakia," *Artscanada*, June 1970, pp. 2–78. Artistic director of the rock band The Plastic People of the Universe.

Juráček, Pavel (1935–). Movie director, film scenarist, dramaturge, who helped create the "New Wave" of Czech cinema in the 1960s. Lives in West Germany.

Kabeš, Petr (1941–). Poet, journalist, editor of literary magazine, *Sešity* (1966–68).

Kainar, Josef (1917–). Poet, playwright, writer, song composer; member of Group 42.

Kantůrková, Eva (1930–). Journalist and writer. *My Companions in the Bleak House* (Woodstock, New York: Overlook, 1988); "In the Middle of Bohemia" in *The Writing on the Wall*, Antonín Liehm and Peter Kussi, eds. (New York: Karz-Cohl, 1983).

Glossary

Klíma, Ivan (1931–). Writer, *Literární Noviny* editor. *Games* in *Drama-Contemporary: Czechoslovakia,* Marketa Goetz-Stankiewicz, ed. (New York: Performing Arts Journal, 1985); *My Merry Mornings* (London: Readers International, 1987).

Kliment, Alexander (1929–). Dramaturge, poet, and novelist.

Knížák, Milan (1940–). Artist, performance artist; head of the Academy of Fine Arts, Prague.

Kohout, Pavel (1928–). Poet, playwright, since 1978 resident in Vienna. *From the Diary of a Counterrevolutionary* (New York: McGraw-Hill, 1972); *The Hangwoman* (New York: Putnam, 1981); *Poor Murderer* (New York: Viking, 1977); *White Book* (New York: Braziller, 1977); "A Feuilleton on Feuilletons," "Bebra," and "Trouble," in *The Writing on the Wall,* Antonín Liehm and Peter Kussi, eds. (New York: Karz-Cohl, 1983).

Kolář, Jiří (1914–). Poet and visual artist, since late 1970s resident in Paris. "Selected Poems," *Cross Currents* 8 (1989); also various anthologies and exhibition catalogues.

Komeda, Vendelín. Historian, now living in West Germany.

Kopta, Petr (1927–). Translator, poet, playwright.

Kosík, Karel (1926–). Philosopher, historian of Czech culture and art. In 1968, Professor at Charles University, and member of Communist Party politburo.

Kramář, Karel (1860–1937). Czech politician. Led the domestic underground struggle against Austria during the first World War; later became head of the conservative National Democratic Party.

Krejča, Otomar. Director of *Theatre Za Branou* (Theatre Beyond the Gate).

Kriegel, Frantisek. Politician in Czechoslovak goverment under Dubček; signatory of Charter 77.

Kuběna, Jiri [pseudonym of Jiří Paukert] (1936–). Poet, member of *Tvář* writers' circle.

Glossary

Kundera, Milan (1929–). Prose writer, since 1975 resident in France. *The Book of Laughter and Forgetting* (New York: Knopf, 1980); *The Farewell Party* (New York: Knopf, 1976); *The Joke* (New York: Harper & Row, 1982); *Laughable Loves* (New York: Knopf, 1974); *Life Is Elsewhere* (New York: Knopf, 1974); *The Unbearable Lightness of Being* (New York: Harper & Row, 1984); *The Art of the Novel* (New York: Grove, 1986); various essays.

Kuron, Jacek. Activist in Solidarity trade union and in Committe for the Defense of the Workers (KOR). Minister of Labour in the present Polish goverment.

Landovský, Pavel (1936–). Actor and playwright, a founder of Prague's Činoherní Klub; since 1978 member of acting ensemble of Vienna's Burgtheater. *Detour* in *DramaContemporary: Czechoslovakia,* Marketa Goetz-Stankiewicz, ed. (New York: Performing Arts Journal, 1985); "Things Have a Habit of Going their Own Way" in *The Writing on the Wall,* Antonín Liehm and Peter Kussi, eds. (New York: Karz-Cohl, 1983).

Lederer, Jiří (1922–1983). Journalist, until 1969 reporter for *Lidové Noviny* and *Reportér;* spent 1972, 1974, 1977–1981 in prison, after which he emigrated.

Liehm, Antonín Jaroslav (1924–). Film and literary critic, publicist, member of editorial board of *Literární Noviny* and editor of *Letres Internationale.* Since 1968 resident in the United States and France. (With Mira Liehm) *The Most Important Art* (Berkeley: University of California Press, 1977); *The Politics of Culture* (New York: Grove, 1968); *Closely Watched Films* (White Plains, New York: International Arts & Sciences Press, 1974); numerous essays.

Linhartová, Věra (1938–). Writer and art historian, since 1968 resident in Paris. "The Room" in *Czech and Slovak Short Stories,* Jeanne Nemcova, ed. and trans. (New York: Oxford University Press, 1967).

Lopatka, Jan (1940–). Literary critic and editor.

Macourek, Miloš (1926–). Scenarist, dramaturge, poet. Since 1959 associated with *Divadlo Na Zábradlí* (Theatre on the Balustrade).

Majerová, Marie (1882–?). Writer, member of Communist Party of Czechoslovakia, journalist.

Glossary

Michnik, Adam. Activist, founding member of the Committee for the Defense of the Workers (KOR) in Poland. *Letters From Prison* (University of California Press, 1985). Editor of *Gazeta Wyborcza*, the first independent Polish daily.

Mlynář, Zdeněk (1930–). Politician and journalist, in 1968 member of Alexander Dubček's Central Committee. Since 1977 resident in Austria. *Nightfrost in Prague* (New York: Karz-Cohl, 1980).

Morgenstern, Christian (1871–1941). German poet, author of mystical, grotesque, humorous poetry.

Nápravník, Milan (1931–). Surrealist poet, since 1968 resident in West Germany, editor for Deutsche Welle and Deutschlandfunk [German radio].

Němec, Jiří (1932–). Psychologist, essayist, since 1981 resident in Austria.

Ornest, Ota (1913–). Stage director. "Czech Drama Since the Second World War," in Jindřich Honzl, ed. *The Czechoslovak Theatre* (Prague: Orbis, 1948). Tried for subversion in 1977 and sentenced to three and a half years in prison.

Pachman, Luděk (1924–). Journalist, author of books on chess. Lives in West Germany.

Páral, Vladimír. Writer, *Catapult* (Highland Park, New Jersey: Catbird Press, 1989).

Patočka, Jan (1907–1977). Philosopher, student of Husserl and Heidegger, died after a police interrogation about his work as Charter 77 spokesperson. "European Culture," *Cross Currents* 3 (1984).

Peroutka, Ferdinand (1895–1978). Journalist, writer, editor-in-chief of *Přítomnost* and *Dnešek;* 1939–1945 in Buchenwald; in exile after 1948. Worked for Radio Free Europe; died in New York.

Pilař, Jan (1917–). Poet, translator; in 1949 secretary of the Union of Czechoslovak Writers; from 1954 editor-in-chief of *Lidové Noviny.*

Pištora, Jiří (1932–1970). Poet, literary critic, essayist, editor of *Tvář* magazine (1963–64).

Glossary

Procházka, Jan (1929–1971). Film scenarist and prose writer. *Long Live the Republic* (Garden City, New York: Doubleday, 1973).

Pujmanová, Marie (1893–1958). Writer, essayist, journalist, poet.

Rádl, Emanuel (1873–1942). Professor of philosophy at the Charles University of Prague; a student of T. G. Masaryk.

Šabata, Jaroslav (1927–). Onetime prominent Party member, later became Charter 77 spokesperson.

Šafařík, Josef (1907–). Philosopher and essayist.

Schauer, Gordon Hubert (1862–1892). Literary critic of Czech-German extraction, editor of Otto's encyclopedia.

Scheinpflugová, Olga (1902–1968). Actress and writer, wife of writer Karel Čapek.

Seifert, Jaroslav (1901–1985). Poet, winner of 1984 Nobel Prize in Literature. *The Plague Monument* (Silver Spring: Arts and Science Society, 1980); *Selected Poems of Jaroslav Seifert* (New York: Macmillan, 1986); "Being a Poet Means Taking a Stand" in *A Besieged Culture*, A. Heneka et al., eds. (Stockholm: Charta 77 Foundation, 1985); widely anthologized.

Sidon, Karol (1942–). Film scenarist, author of radio and television plays, journalist; editor of *Literární Listy* (1968–69).

Skála, Ivan (1922–). Poet, literary critic, translator. Head of Czechoslovak Union of Writers (1959–64); member of politburo of Czechoslovak Communist party and MP.

Škvorecký, Josef (1924–). Prose writer, since 1969 professor at University of Toronto and, with his wife, Zdena Salivarová, publisher of Czech émigré literature. *All the Bright Young Men and Women* (Toronto: Peter Martin, 1971); *The Bass Saxophone* (New York: Knopf, 1979); *The Cowards* (New York: Grove, 1970); *The Engineer of Human Souls* (New York: Knopf, 1984); *Dvorak in Love* (New York: Knopf, 1987); various essays; widely anthologized.

Slánský, Rudolf (1901–1952). General Secretary of Czechoslovak Communist Party; tried for being the head of an anti-state conspiracy and executed in 1952.

The Šmidras. A group of artists in Prague during the sixties and seventies.

Smrkovský, Josef. Politician, member of Czechoslovak goverment during Prague Spring of 1968.

Steigerwald, Karel (1945–). Playwright and film scenarist.

Suchý, Jiří (1931–). Actor, singer, poet, writer, member of Balustrade and Semafor theatres, teamed with composer Jiří Šlitr (Š & S) to carry on the tradition of Voskovec and Werich's (V & W) Liberated Theatre. One of the most important theatrical figures of the 1960s. "The Song of Dr. Smith" in *New Writing in Czechoslovakia*, George Theiner, ed. (Baltimore: Penguin, 1969).

Text-appeals. Evenings of jazz, poetry, and prose modeled on similar events held in "bohemian" circles in New York and San Francisco in the 1950s. The work, read by the authors, was usually written especially for the performance.

Tigrid, Pavel (1917–). Journalist, editor-in-chief of *Vývoj,* associated with Radio Free Europe, publisher of émigré cultural journal *Svědectví* in Paris.

Topol, Josef (1935–). Playwright, dramaturge of Theatre Behind the Gate under artistic director Otomar Krejča.

Trefulka, Jan (1929–). Literary critic and prose writer.

Třešňák, Vlasta (1950–). Underground singer, painter, and writer, now living in West Germany. "Once Upon a Time" in *The Writing on the Wall,* Antonín Liehm and Peter Kussi, eds. (New York: Karz-Cohl, 1983).

Tříska, Jan (1936–). Actor, one of the founders of Theatre Behind the Gate; since 1977 resident in United States. "East Europe? West? Both? Neither?" in *Cross Currents,* 1982.

Uhde, Milan (1936–). Poet, playwright, literary and theatre critic, editor of *Host do Domu* magazine (1960–69).

Uhl, Petr (1941–). Student leader, journalist, and self-described "revolutionary socialist"; in 1960s published (under the pseudonym Vladimir Skalsky) a critical study of socialism. Tried with Havel for subversion and sentenced to five years in a maximum security prison in Mírov.

Urbánek, Zdeněk (1917–). Translator and essayist, best known for his translations of Shakespeare's plays.

Vaculík, Ludvík (1926–). Journalist, writer. *The Axe* (New York: Harper & Row, 1973); *The Guinea Pigs* (New York: Third Press, 1973); *A Cup of Coffee With My Interrogator* (London: Readers International, 1987); widely anthologized.

Valenta, Edvard (1901–1978). Journalist, writer, editor of *Lidové Noviny*; worked for Peroutka's *Dnešek*.

Vladislav, Jan (1923–). Poet, essayist, translator, prose writer, author of books for children. Editor-in-chief of *Světová Literatura* (World Literature), 1969–70. Living in France since 1981.

Vohryzek, Josef (1926–). Literary critic, translator, prose writer. Editor at Československy Spisovatel publishing house (1964–72).

VONS. The Czech acronym for the Committee to Defend the Unjustly Persecuted, which was formed in 1978 as an offshoot of Charter 77 to monitor the cases of people who were indicted or imprisoned for expressing their beliefs or who were victims of abuses by the police and the courts.

Voskovec, Jiří (1905–1981). Actor, dramatist, song writer, film scenarist. Teamed with Jan Werich on the stage of the avant-garde *Osvobozené Divadlo* (Liberated Theatre) in Prague. Became a well-known actor in New York after the war.

Vostrý, Jaroslav. Dramaturge of Činoherní Klub theatre until 1968 and after 1989.

Vyskočil, Ivan (1929–). Experimental prose writer. "The Incredible Rise of Albert Uruk" in *New Writing in Czechoslovakia*, George Theiner, ed. (Baltimore: Penguin, 1969).

Werich, Jan (1905–1980). Actor, writer, with Jiří Voskovec founded Liberated Theatre in 1927; 1939–1945 resident in United States; in 1960s artistic director of ABC Theatre in Prague.

Glossary

Zábrana, Jan (1931–1984). Poet, translator from Russian (Esenin, Pasternak, Mandelstam, Tsvetaeva, and others) and English (Ferlinghetti, Corso, Ginsburg, and others).

Zahradníček, Jan (1905–1960). Poet, translator, Catholic Journalist.

Index

Index